# POWER READ THE BIBLE

## A COMPANION GUIDE FOR YOUR 60-DAY JOURNEY

# JEFF ANDERSON

*Dedicated to the participants in my first 60-day Bible reading class at Fellowship Bible Church in Tulsa.*

*Your hunger and enthusiasm convinced me people really do want to read the Bible – all of it! This companion tool is a response to your shining example.*

# TABLE OF CONTENTS

# INTRODUCTION

You want to read the Bible – cover to cover? Well, you can!

Not only can you read the full Bible. You can understand it and truly enjoy the experience. And did I mention you can read it in 60 days, about an hour a day?

If there's anything I've learned about Bible reading, it's this. Few Christians have read it completely. But many want to. They're just not sure they can. Or they've never been encouraged to do so.

Many have been burned by failed 365-day reading plans, only to crash somewhere by February... or sooner. Or if they made it past that point, the satisfaction of reading was offset by the disappointment that they didn't really understand what they had read.

I want you to know, your desire to read the Bible is admirable (and noticed by God). And I want to help you complete the experience.

Whether you're reading the Bible for the first time, or you're a life long Bible reader looking for a fresh experience, you're going to love this 60-day journey.

Here's how this book will help you in your Bible-reading journey:

1.  Direction – Our focus is the overall narrative of the Bible. This is not deep dive Bible study. By keeping a big picture perspective, you'll see the Bible open up in ways you have likely never seen before.

2.  Mindset – This approach requires a fast-paced reading style. I call it "Power Reading." It's a different style of Bible engagement. If you're willing to try, you'll find

that the big picture view of scripture is not only possible, but more attainable, from a cranked-up reading pace.

3.  Encouragement – This book is not the kind of reading plan where I do some calendar math and walk away. I'm with you for 60 days, providing a fresh word of encouragement and perspective as you stay on the path. I'm like your white water rafting guide. We're in the raft together, with oars in the water. We're both getting wet.

This book is a resource guide. I'll explain the idea of the 60-day read and help you get started, then you can use this tool to document your journey.

This 60-day power reading approach is tried and tested. I've experienced the journey with a live class setting. And I've done so with thousands of online participants.

This journey is not a system or a gimmick or a fancy method that comes and goes like the latest diet trend. It's straight-up Bible reading. And it will require a commitment from you.

There's no motivational speech to wind you up like a read-a-thon contestant. I know you're already hungry. You wouldn't be in this book if you weren't.

I've seen teenagers embrace the plan, as well as grandparents; working moms and dads have succeeded, as well as busy stay-at-home parents.

If you're tired of being one of those Christians who have never read the Bible, or if you're simply looking for an adventurous Bible read experience, take a deep breath.

Now is your opportunity.

# CHAPTER 1

## HOW DID THIS 60-DAY BIBLE READ COME ABOUT?

I always wanted to read the entire Bible. It seemed like something every Christian should do. I tried multiple times early in my Christian journey, but encountered a familiar set of challenges.

**The easy-hard paradox:** I mostly tried the 365-day plans, and failed. It's especially defeating when you know the goal really isn't daunting at all (*Come on Jeff, it's just a few chapters a day!*) The strange truth is, it's so easy that it's hard.

**Confusion and boredom:** When I did read, I didn't understand everything I was reading. This felt pointless. But how dare I call any portions of God's text uninteresting or difficult or... boring? (Feels like blasphemy!)

**The pass-fail proposition:** Most Bible reading plans are "all or nothing." You either finish the plan, or you fail to read the entire Bible. It's hard to find a silver lining when you crash in Leviticus.

## DO ANY OF THESE RESONATE WITH YOUR EXPERIENCES?

Well, years ago I came across a 30-day reading plan that was proposed by my good friend, Bruce Ammons, a pastor in Texas. Bruce showed me that the Bible really is readable –

and can be read in a compressed period of time.

After my first 30-day read, I took a short break. Then I started again and read it in 40 days. In roughly three months, I read the Bible twice.

The number of days doesn't matter. It's the power reading approach that makes all the difference in the world. For purposes of this book, and based on experience guiding others, I recommend this 60-day reading plan.

Here are three benefits from Power Reading (further explained in Chapter 4) that flipped each of my prior frustrations on its head.

## #1 We Need Big Goals

I tried one-year plans before, only to veer off course somewhere by February. I always considered the goal too difficult. But the real reason for my failure was that the 365-day goal was too easy!

Sounds crazy, doesn't it? But think about it.

Often in life, goals that are easy are not worth doing. That's not to say that reading the Bible in a year is not a worthwhile goal. It is! But the daily reading demands of the one-year plan are so small that we often don't embrace the exercise or take it seriously.

People will embrace big goals. Marathon running, Couch-to-5K programs, 30-day body detox plans. Seemingly daunting challenges lead to greater success than trying to tackle smaller, comfortable goals.

The refreshing truth is this. You *can* read the Bible in far less than a year. And you can benefit from it too (that's the whole point, and we'll discuss this more later).

Since my experience, I've been encouraging and leading others through the journey. The consensus discovery for most everyone is the same: it's far easier to read large quantities for a focused season (of weeks or months) than to read a little bit each day for a long stretch.

## #2 We Need the Big Picture

The Bible was not written to entertain us. (Yes, there are some great stories that make up one overall, grand story). But there's also some very dry text—genealogies, census records, geographical data, weird laws and customs, and some seemingly cryptic poetry.

When doing a 60-day Bible read, we don't try to understand everything. Instead we read to catch the big picture. Once we know the overall narrative, we can learn to power through the tough text patches along the way.

We don't slow down to study the Old Testament laws or details of the tabernacle. We're tracking the overarching, end-to-end storyline of the Bible—the story of The Seed, 4,000 years of biblical history in which a human seed travels through roughly sixty-four generations.

With a compact read like the 60-day schedule, the big picture takes shape quickly. Instead of taking weeks or months to get through Deuteronomy (and losing focus of the big picture), the 60-day plan helps us through a time-lapse view.

We clear Genesis through Deuteronomy (the first five books) in just ten days. We read the entire New Testament in just two weeks.

With focus on the big picture and a brisk reading pace, you'll be surprised just how much you *will* understand.

## #3 We Need Lots of Grace

The 60-day read is a grace-filled plan. That may sound ironic for such an aggressive schedule, but it's true. You suit the plan to fit you.

I provide a 60-day reading schedule. From my experience with groups, I'm reminded that life doesn't roll the same for everyone. Life happens, right? You may get behind. And that's fine.

A small minority of the readers are die-hard goal-trotters who will finish in exactly 60-days. (Wow!) A much larger group will float across the finish line between sixty and seventy days. (Still very awesome.) Some will take longer, eighty or ninety days. (Again, what an amazing accomplishment.)

A small minority decide that "power reading" isn't for them so they stay on a slower track, yet still reading more of the Bible than they have before, gaining new insights and tracking the big picture themes presented in this book.

The key is that this is *your* plan. You set the goals and the targets. I will share some strategies for managing the pace, and some catch–up techniques for the "Type A" goal-setters.

The only rule I have for this plan is: No Guilt Allowed!

# CHAPTER 2

## REASONS WE DON'T READ THE BIBLE

Before we dive into the power-read strategies and the 60-day reading plan, lets talk about some of the hurdles to Bible reading. Why is Bible engagement declining for Christian families?

My wife and I have four children, with our oldest in college and youngest in elementary school. Helping them develop their own walk with God is on our minds—a lot!

So are questions about why so many young people are walking away from faith, and why parents often have a distant relationship with God.

I'm called to guide my own family, and help other believers walk with God. I've seen all kinds of programs, books, and solutions offered. All sound wonderful, but seem to fall short.

And there are plenty of explanations about why young people are drifting from faith – it's culture... it's media... it's parenting styles... it's ineffective youth ministry.

I kept coming back to an answer that was so obvious... I almost missed it. The Bible.

It's no secret biblical literacy is on decline (and this includes for Christian families.) Every major researcher on faith trends seems to be reporting it.

# BUT WHY?

The Bible is our only unchanging, tangible lifeline to our faith. Its words are the truest, and most transferable expression of God.

Only the Bible levels the playing field for anyone to approach God.

In many ways, the words are the closest we can get to our Creator, and the only way faith transfers from one generation to the next.

There are plenty of Bible substitutes on the market—products, apps, and topical books. They are not the answer. We have access to bazillions. Cartoons won't build our faith, movies won't renew our minds, and seminars won't feed our hearts. Not like the Bible does.

## The Bible text is alive.

So why do we settle for being once-removed from the source? Why aren't we meeting God through His Word?

People don't read the Bible because they don't like it. But... People don't like the Bible because they don't read it.

Here are seven reasons people are not reading the Bible today.

## 1. The Bible is Optional

After all, we have TV, internet, and plenty of "wise" voices touting answers. The faith message has been oversimplified with trite expressions:

Love God, love people.

*Why do I need to read that dusty book when I have a four-word synopsis?*

Many people see more verses of scripture on Facebook memes than in their Bible. And to them, Facebook replaces the Bible.

## 2. Many Church Leaders Don't Expect Us to Read the Bible

I didn't say leaders don't *want* people to read the Bible, they don't *expect* it.

How can we tell?

Are you encouraged to bring your Bible to church?

When our kids were babies and toddlers, we didn't expect them to feed themselves, or even know how. So we fed them little bites of baby food. Eventually we expected them to feed themselves, and even make their own meals.

Expository pastors are content to feed a spoonful at a time. Thematic-preaching pastors enjoy bringing a topical flavor-of-the-month. Both have a place, but shouldn't we be encouraged (and expected) to do some self-feeding at home?

College professors expect their students to read the textbook outside of class. But many pastors don't expect the same of their flocks.

## 3. Overselling Mission and Vision

An unintended consequence of church branding and mission statements is constant preaching of vision, and funding for mission.

In a growing number of churches, vision has replaced discipleship. The A-B-C's (attendance, baptisms, cash) are measurable... spiritual growth (which includes Bible literacy) is difficult to assess.

Even when "discipleship" is programmed, there's little or no emphasis on personal Bible reading. (See #2)

## 4. Google Faith

We can Google a Bible verse, or blog about a verse, any time we want. So why read what's around it?

100 million people have downloaded the YouVersion Bible app. I celebrate that fact.

My question is, with accessibility to scripture climbing by the day, why is faith and Bible engagement declining?

Since we can always Google the Bible when we "need" it, we rarely read the book.

## 5. Failure

For some, even thinking about that leather-bound book triggers memories of personal failure. And who wants to be reminded of that?! As I mentioned earlier, if you've ever tried a 365-day read, you know what I'm talking about. For others, disappointing and confusing experiences reading the Bible have triggered resignation (keep that book away from me).

## 6. Your Parents Don't Read the Bible

I'm talking to your kids, now. ;-)

(Parents, if you don't read it, your kids won't, statistically speaking. If you've given up, your children may never begin.)

## 7. Bible Bullies

Sincere believers are often made to believe, overtly and covertly, that they are not smart or educated enough to truly understand the Bible.

Sounds like something Martin Luther railed against 500 years ago! (We're at the 500th anniversary of the beginning of the reformation in 1517, by the way.) He went on to translate a version of the Bible in their language so more people could read it. Like others before and after, he was persecuted for giving such a "lofty" book to lowly people.

Today, some bestselling authors make followers believe that without the benefit of their education and knowledge of "historical context" they can't possibly understand the Bible accurately. When Bible teachers proudly explain how the Greek or Hebrew word means something different than what you've always believed it to say, reader confidence is crushed.

That's enough with the excuses. Let's shift to what I trust is really on our hearts – reasons we want to read the Bible.

# CHAPTER 3

## REASONS WE SHOULD READ THE BIBLE

Here are some positive reasons why we *want* to read the Bible.

### 1. Check off the list

Yeah, that's right. Read the Bible and check the box. There's nothing wrong with that.

For Christians, reading the entire Bible should be on the short list of lifetime spiritual goals. Don't listen to those voices that suggest Christian disciplines are legalistic and harmful. Sure, anything can err on that side at times. But we're talking about something you want to do, right?

So if you want to read the Bible because you never have, welcome! This 60-day adventure is for you. And by the way, I don't believe reading the Bible will be a one-and-done experience for you. You'll want to do it again.

### 2. Seek God

This reason alone is sufficient for us all. If we read God's Word, we seek Him. If we don't read God's Word, we're choosing to not seek Him.

When God says, "You will seek me and find me when you seek me with all your heart" (Jeremiah 29:13), I don't know how this is possible apart from consuming God's Word like food.

## 3. Stay Anchored

As mentioned earlier, teens and young adults are drifting from faith today. And a central reason is Biblical illiteracy. Christians don't know their Bibles, and therefore, Christian faith is shallow. The less you know about faith, the more vulnerable you are to drift. Deep knowledge of the faith is harder to uproot. Beginning and staying in the Word keeps you anchored in the faith.

Content is powerful. When I was young, I remember seminars at church warning parents and teenagers of the dangers of heavy metal rock music. Today a similar concern is the devastating effects of pornography.

On the flip side, content can be powerfully good. Saturating your mind with things of the Spirit (God's Word) keeps us anchored in the faith.

## 4. Get Rich!

Solomon, the wisest man ever said that the most precious commodity known to man – was wisdom. More valuable than gold and silver is wisdom (and knowledge and understanding.) All three come from reading the Bible.

## 5. Be Relevant and Relatable

When you read the Bible completely and regularly, it's amazing how current and relevant the words become.

You turn on Christian radio and hear a Bible message—and realize you just read the related text last week.

Or you hear a sermon at church—and the text is a passage you read a few days earlier. You hear a news report on TV or online, and it reminds you of a theme you've been catching in your Bible reading.

Consuming large quantities of scripture on a regular basis

affords you ongoing teaching moments for your family, and relate-ability with both believers and non-believers in your network.

Active Bible readers are not like ostriches with their heads in the sand (the Bible). They're not ignorant of world affairs. Bible readers are informed citizens, gaining a wealth of wisdom and knowledge to make sound judgments about the everyday world in which we live.

## 6. Faith Restarts

Moses instructed the Israelites to teach the law to their families every day. But he knew that everyone needs a fresh restart now and then. That's why he instructed the congregation to read the entire book of the law every seven years.

Joshua triggered a restart reading as soon as they crossed the Jordan River (Joshua 8). King Josiah ordered a restart when the dust-covered book of the law was discovered in the temple (2 Kings 22). Ezra and Nehemiah instituted some restart reading sessions when they rebuilt the temple and the walls (Nehemiah 8).

> *We all need faith restarts—fresh opportunities*
> *to recharge our faith batteries.*

The need for a faith refresher was exactly what set me on this journey of "power reading" the scriptures. My faith was dry, my prayers were stalled and my time in God's Word was lacking. So I jumped into a 30-day Bible read and found that spark I needed.

Perhaps a faith restart is exactly what you need at this time in your faith journey.

## 7. Because You Can!

Read the Bible because you can... it's more doable than you think. With a few tweaks in your schedule and priorities, and a hungry heart, you can read the Bible in 60 days!

## WHY READ THE BIBLE IN 60 DAYS?

- Big goals are more appealing and engage our hearts
- Gain familiarity with the Bible's big picture
- Make the Bible "smaller"
- Wake up your soul when you need a spiritual boost
- Kick that feeling of guilt that you don't know the Bible like you wish you did
- Put the Bible back at the center of your home (you will carry your bible around all the time for 60 days)
- Your family will see you in God's Word
- A spiritual detox is good for us (time away from media, etc.)
- Show God you're hungry and you want to better understand His Word

# CHAPTER 4

## WHAT IS POWER READING?

"Power Reading" is a different kind of Bible engagement. It's the opposite of scripture memory or meditation or deep dive Bible study, which all require intense focus on a limited portion of text.

Power reading is sort of like watching an NFL football game in fifteen minutes. I'm told that an actual NFL game can be viewed in only eleven minutes. The rest of the three-plus hours of network programming is time in the huddle, calling plays, and just running off the clock... it's commercials... it's the camera panning the crowd, the sidelines, the cheerleaders or Jerry Jones in his suite.

The Power Read is a "keep moving" reading experience. As already mentioned, the goal isn't to understand everything. The benefits are different—familiarity, big-picture view, making the Bible smaller and less intimidating.

For many, it's a first time to experience the full Bible at once. And for everyone, a fresh, spiritual reset for the soul.

It takes practice to learn to read quickly. The natural tendency is to slow down for greater reading comprehension. But there are lots of chapters to cover each day. Discipline is necessary to keep moving.

# POWER READING IS MORE ART THAN SCIENCE

You'll learn to figure out what works for you as you start reading. The first week of the reading plan, you'll get a feel for how much time you'll need to invest each day. I suggest starting with one hour of reading each day. You may need more. Or you might need less.

As a general rule, read quickly! However, some sections should be read more carefully and less rapidly than others. And other sections will be like weaving in and out of traffic to get to the next destination.

To help you with your reading pace, I've provided a Pace Chart that's imbedded in the Reading Plan. Take a look at Chapter 7.

# I RECOMMEND THREE DIFFERENT SPEEDS:

**Speed 1** – This is the slowest speed, yet still what I consider "comfortably fast." You're reading quickly, sounding out most every word in your mind as your eyes float across the page.

**Speed 3** –This is the fastest speed, sort of like high-paced skimming. It's rushed reading. You're not necessarily giving attention to every word. Your eyes float down the page (or screen) as much as from left to right.

**Speed 2** – This speed is in between 1 and 3. You be the judge.

I've provided space for taking notes on each day's reading. Use this space to write down passages that stand out, as reminders to return after you've completed the read. The box on each page is there to write a theme, or themes, so you can quickly refer to them later.

## LET'S LOOK AT AN EXAMPLE:

Referring to the 60-day reading plan in Chapter 7, you'll notice Days 1, 2, and 3 are "Speed 1" texts. The account of Genesis is foundational history. It might warrant some of the slowest reading of your entire plan.

On Day 4 you're in Exodus. (Pretty cool, huh?) After the Israelite jailbreak from Egypt, the biblical narrative gets off track a bit and enters into a section of laws, customs and tent tabernacle minutia – which, for the reader, means picking up the pace.

So beginning in Exodus 21 (after the Ten Commandments), I shift from Speed 1 to Speed 3. Burning rubber through the pages.

Some sections I have marked by two or three different speeds (like Psalms and Proverbs). That's so you can pick your own speed.

Remember, it's your plan. You determine the rules. The Pace Chart is simply an optional tool. If you want to read the entire Bible in Speed 1 and pronounce every word in your mind, go for it.

Again, finding your relative reading pace will be a work in progress the first few days.


## SOME FAQS ABOUT POWER READING

### 1. *Isn't Power Reading like cheating? I mean, can it really be considered Bible-reading?*

Cheating? Who said there are rules for Bible reading?

Power reading is a reading mindset. You don't have to fully

grasp or comprehend everything you're reading. The mindset offers freedom and peace of mind to move quickly through the Bible.

God's blessings are no less because of a faster reading pace. In fact, because of the coverage and the big picture discoveries that come with it, power reading has some significant benefits you can't get any other way. But you'll need to try it for yourself.

### 2. What if I'm the "Type A" kind of reader and want to read and sound every word in my mind?

OK, honey... you can do it that way. (That's my wife I'm talking to, by the way. She's admittedly a slow reader and doesn't like to cruise through the pages at a rushed pace. So she takes her time and checks off every word in her mind. She's okay if the schedule gets away from her. If she doesn't finish till 90 days or even much more, she's fine with that. So find your style and comfort zone.)

### 3. Can I listen to the Bible on audio?

Absolutely! Remember, there are no rules – except for the ones that you set for yourself. Some folks tell me they listened to the Bible during their daily commute to work and it helped to break up the reading portions. And if you want to listen to all of it, go for it.

Personally I'm a visual learner more than an auditory one, so I prefer reading the text. And it's also easier to highlight the Bible and make notes for future reference while reading.

[As a hint for the audio listeners, many audio formats allow you to speed up the voice a bit to move it along more quickly. Try it!]

### 4. What do I do if I get off track of the schedule? Like WAY off track.

Hey, I get this. Life happens. If you get behind, here are my personal strategies (yes, I get behind too):

i. **Adjust your goal.** If your 60-day plan turns into 75, or 90, or 120 days, that's still awesome! I finished my second Bible power-read in 40 days. No, I did not have a 40-day plan. I simply fell behind 10 days on my 30-day plan.

ii. **Skip the hard sections.** If you get way off track and feel discouraged, then come up for air and fast-forward to a new section of the reading schedule. Maybe you're stuck in the Major Prophets. You might decide to jump ahead to the Minor Prophets and come back later to the sections you passed over. (Remember, you set the rules.)

iii. **Crunch time.** If you are determined that you are going to finish the Bible in 60 days, then buckle down and do what it takes. I often use weekend cram sessions to catch up. I've even heard of folks taking a vacation day from work to do some volume reading. If the goal of completing the Bible read is that important to you personally, there are ways to buckle down and power through to get caught up. Be creative.

### 5. What if I'm sort of a freak and I want to get ahead of the plan.

Do it! Don't let the plan slow you down. If the lure of a 30-day challenge fits you, then just double the assigned reading and go for it. Depending on your hunger and personal reading style, you might prefer a more intense reading pace in exchange for a more compressed calendar.

When doing a 30-day pace, start by planning to invest at least two hours of reading per day. You can adjust once you find your pace and rhythm.

### 6.  Any cautions for young families?

If you're married, be sensitive to what this challenge means for your family. I've seen cases where both spouses read the entire Bible according to plan, even with small needy children at home. My hat is off to those fine examples!

For my wife and me, it has not worked so beautifully. We don't do well with both of us simultaneously power-reading on an aggressive plan. While it's easy for me to slip out to the coffee shop with my Bible and leave her home with the kids, this doesn't serve her very well.

And remember, just because you're not power reading through a 60-day plan does not mean you can't be in the Word.

Power reading is simply *one* way to engage the Bible during special seasons.

It is not *the only* way.

Another note for families: I've been pleasantly surprised by the number of young teenagers who have taken on the 60-day plan, often setting the pace for the parents! Another reminder to us that the Bible truly is readable.

### 7.  What happens when the journey turns dry?

When it comes to prayer, fasting, Bible reading, etc., there's work and sacrifice involved. This 60-day journey is amazingly doable – but it's not without great effort and discipline. And some days will be less energizing than others.

Always remember, as you read you are spending time with God ("the Word was God" John 1:1). Take pauses to say "You see me, don't you God?"

You are showing God you value His Word. By taking an hour to read the Bible, you are taking an hour from something else.

Be encouraged by the story of the Ethiopian eunuch in Acts Chapter 8. He was diligently reading through the scrolls of Isaiah but struggling to understand what he was reading. God saw his faithfulness and prepared a special encounter for him.

God notices your sacrifice and efforts to seek Him in this way. If you find the routine becomes stale, don't despair. Gut through it.

While Bible engagement is a lifetime journey, "power reading" is for special seasons. Embrace this season.


### 8. What if I've started the plan but the timing is just not right for me?

Starting over is OK. If you launch into the plan and determine the time is just not right, step aside—with no guilt!

Get back on the plan when the timing is better for you.

# CHAPTER 5

## GETTING THE MOST OUT OF THIS
## COMPANION GUIDE

It's almost time to begin reading. Here's a quick checklist to help you get started, and tips on how to use this book.

### 1. Select Your Bible

- I recommend a Bible with no study notes or commentaries. These slow down reading and can often distract you from the main themes.
- Consider reading a new Bible or one that does not have your notes or markings from the past (not crucial, just an idea... or an excuse if you want a fresh, new Bible)
- Choose a readable translation (like ESV, NIV, NASB, etc.) but avoid paraphrases (The Message, etc.). If you've done a Bible read-through before, perhaps try a new translation for fun.
- Large print, easy-to-read font is helpful to the eyes.
- Personally, I prefer a physical-Bible in my hands for this experience, with a highlighter and a pen nearby. I have completed a power-read on my Bible phone app and that has benefits also. It's always in my pocket and available whenever I have unexpected time on my hands.

(In the space below, note which Bible format or particular Bible you are going to be reading.)

_____

_____

_____

_____

## 2. Set Your Reading Plan and Schedule

- Set a start date, and your reading goal. Jot it down on the lines below. If you are determined to read it in 60-days, it helps to put it in writing. (*i.e. I plan to read the Bible in 60 days, beginning on January 10th and finishing March 10th.*)

- To start, set aside an hour a day to find your pace. For some readers, it might be less. Note your plan below (*i.e. I plan to wake up at 6am and begin reading for 45 minutes. If needed, I'll find another 15 minutes during lunch hour*).

- Now fill in the 60-day reading plan calendar in Chapter 7, based on your scheduled start date.

- Using lines below, note any particular calendar events that will require mindful planning on your part (i.e. work travel or project deadlines, vacations, holidays, etc.)

_____

_____

_____

_____

_____

## 3. Keep a Journal

- Keep your Bible and this guidebook with you during the day. Prime reading opportunities are often unexpected (waiting room for doctor visits, carpool pick-up lines, and time between appointments).
- Read each day's encouragement before you begin the day's read.
- As you read, jot down any notes, questions, observations for later reflection. This way you can keep on reading and save the reflection and follow-up study for later.

## 4. Track Key Themes

On page 2 of each day's reading is a small box. It's there for you to note key themes which emerge on the passages, but use it for anything that helps you process the reading experience.

We'll explore this more in the next chapter.

# CHAPTER 6

## PICK A THEME

One last idea! This is another tip I learned from my friend, Bruce. Before you begin your read, consider picking a theme of focus, a topic that you'd like to watch for in your reading. It could a single-word theme like:

- Salvation
- Marriage
- Forgiveness
- Rewards
- Grace
- Wisdom
- Money
- Work
- Parenting

The list is endless. Or you could pick a theme that represents a season in your life:

- Choosing to get married
- Decision to take a new job
- Selecting a college or course of study
- Battling depression
- Praying for healing
- Dealing with a wayward child

- Restoring a broken marriage
- Loneliness or isolation

You get the idea.

## USING THE THEME BOX

Once you select your theme, simply read with that theme in mind and look for direct (or even indirect) mention of that theme. As you come across these themes or words in your daily reads, highlight the text in your Bible and note the scripture references in the Theme Box for that day. (You'll find it on the second page of each reading.)

When you complete your 60-day Bible reading journey, you can go back through your notes and review the scripture references and themes you've written in the boxes.

For my first 30-day read, I chose the theme of "wisdom"– specifically, I noted all the mentions of "wisdom", "understanding", "knowledge." For my next power read journey, I selected the theme of "Bible." Of course the word "Bible" is not in the Bible – so my focus was on words like: "word, statutes, laws, commandments, scriptures, scrolls, etc."

Remember, this idea is optional. If it appeals to you and you find it helpful, great. If you prefer to not have a bias in your reading, that's fine too.

And feel free to explore. You can start with a theme and abandon it. Or start without a theme and pick one up along the way.

# My themes are:

# CHAPTER 7

## THE READING PLAN AND TOOLS

On the following four pages you'll find the reading plan. The daily readings are also located on each day's encouragement, which begin in Chapter 8.

## HERE WE GO!

# Read Pace

| Day | Date | 1 (Slower...but still fast) | 2 (In between) | 3 (Fastest) |
|-----|------|------------------------------|-----------------|-------------|
| 1 | | Genesis 1-23 | | |
| 2 | | Genesis 24-39 | | |
| 3 | | Genesis 40 - Exodus 7 | | |
| 4 | | Exodus 8 - 20 | | Exodus 21-27 |
| 5 | | Exodus 32-34 | Exodus 35, 40 | Exodus 28-31, 36-39; Lev 1-7 |
| 6 | | | Lev 10:1-7; 24:10-23 | Leviticus 8-27 |
| 7 | | Numbers 10-17 | Numbers 1-4 | Numbers 5-9 |
| 8 | | Numbers 20-25, 27 | Numbers 18-19; 28-36 | |
| 9 | | Deuteronomy 1-11 | Deuteronomy 12-15 | |
| 10 | | Deuteronomy 31, 34 | Deuteronomy 16-30; 32, 33 | |
| 11 | | Joshua 1-14 | Joshua 15-21 | |
| 12 | | Joshua 23-24; Judges 1-15 | Joshua 22 | |
| 13 | | Judges 16-21; Ruth 1-4; 1 Sam 1-10 | | |
| 14 | | 1 Samuel 11-27 | | |
| 15 | | 1 Samuel 28-31; 2 Samuel 1-15 | | |
| | | See Chapter 4 for instructions, If a segment covers two or more speed categories, you pick the pace | | |

| Day | Date | 1 (Slower...but still fast) | 2 (In between) | 3 (Fastest) |
|-----|------|-----------------------------|----------------|-------------|
| 16 | | 2 Samuel 16-24; 1 Kings 1-5 | | |
| 17 | | 1 Kings 8-14; 17-20 | 1 Kings 6 ,7; 15, 16 | |
| 18 | | | 1 Kings 21-22; 2 Kings 1-14 | |
| 19 | | | 2 Kings 17-25 | 2 Kings 15, 16; 1 Chron 1-5 |
| 20 | | 1 Chronicles 10-23 | | 1 Chron 6-9 |
| 21 | | 1 Chron 28-29; 2 Chron 1,2,5-16 | | 1 Chron 24-27; 2 Chron 3-4 |
| 22 | | 2 Chron 29-31, 34-35 | | 2 Chron 17 -28; 32-33 |
| 23 | | 2 Chron 36, Ezra, Neh 1-7 | | |
| 24 | | Neh 8-13, Esther | Job 1-8 (Speed 1 or 2) | |
| 25 | | | Job 9-34 | |
| 26 | | | Job 35-42, Psalms 1-24 | |
| 27 | | | Psalms 25-54 | |
| 28 | | | Psalms 55-84 | |
| 29 | | | Psalms 85-115 | |
| 30 | | | Psalms 116-150 | |

| Day | Date | 1 (Slower...but still fast) | 2 (In between) | 3 (Fastest) |
|---|---|---|---|---|
| 31 | | | Proverbs 1-19 | |
| 32 | | Ecclesiastes 1-8 | | Proverbs 20-31 |
| 33 | | Eccl 9-12, Songs 1-8, Isaiah 1-9 | | |
| 34 | | | Isaiah 10-31 | |
| 35 | | | Isaiah 32-47 | |
| 36 | | | Isaiah 48-66 | |
| 37 | | | Jeremiah 1-17 | |
| 38 | | Jeremiah 18-34 | | |
| 39 | | | Jeremiah 35-50 | |
| 40 | | | Jer 51-52, Lament 1-5, Ez 1-13 | |
| 41 | | | Ezekiel 14-28 | |
| 42 | | | Ezekiel 29-40 | Ezekiel 41-45 |
| 43 | | Daniel 1-6 | Daniel 7-12 | Ezekiel 46-48 |
| 44 | | | Hosea 1-14, Joel 1-3, Amos 1-9 | |
| 45 | | | Obadiah, Jonah, Micah, Nahum, Habakkuk | |

| Day | Date | 1 (Slower...but still fast) | 2 (In between) | 3 (Fastest) |
|---|---|---|---|---|
| 46 | | | Zephaniah, Haggai, Zechariah, Malachi | |
| 47 | | Matthew 1-17 | | |
| 48 | | Matthew 18-28 | Mark 1-3 | |
| 49 | | | Mark 4-16, Luke 1-3 | |
| 50 | | | Luke 4-16 | |
| 51 | | John 1-5 | Luke 17-24 | |
| 52 | | John 6-17 | | |
| 53 | | John 18-21, Acts 1-8 | | |
| 54 | | Acts 9-28, Romans 1-3 | | |
| 55 | | Romans 4-16, 1 Cor 1-9 | | |
| 56 | | 1 Cor 10-16, 2 Cor 1-13 | | |
| 57 | | Gal., Eph., Phil., Col. | | |
| 58 | | 1&2 Thes., 1&2 Tim, Tit, Phil. | | |
| 59 | | Heb, James, 1&2 Peter | | |
| 60 | | 1/2/3 John, Jude, Revelation | | |

# THE BIBLE'S BIG PICTURE TIMELINE

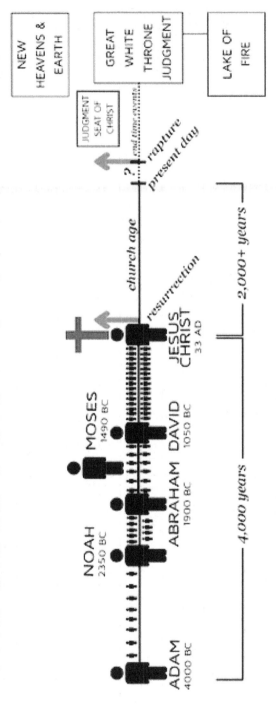

## THE BIBLE IS ABOUT

*the journey of THE SEED that travels through 4,000 years, consisting of 64 generations, connected by 6 key 'resets', focused on 2 resurrection events, which set up 1 final, climactic, redemptive event...*

## THE RECREATION OF THE HEAVENS AND EARTH

# TRACKING "THE SEED"

| | | |
|---|---|---|
| 1. Adam | 23. Judah | 46. Hezekiah |
| 2. Seth | 24. Perez | 47. Manasseh |
| 3. Enos | 25. Hezron | 48. Amon |
| 4. Cainan | 26. Ram | 49. Josiah |
| 5. Mahalaleel | 27. Amminadab | 50. Jehoiakim |
| 6. Jared | 28. Nahshon | 51. Jechoniah |
| 7. Enoch | 29. Salmon | 52. Salathiel |
| 8. Methuselah | 30. Boaz | 53. Zerubbabel |
| 9. Lamech | 31. Obed | 54. Abiud |
| 10. Noah | 32. Jesse | 55. Eliakim |
| 11. Shem | 33. David | 56. Azor |
| 12. Arphaxad | 34. Solomon | 57. Sadoc |
| *Cainan | 35. Rehoboam | 58. Achim |
| 13. Salah | 36. Abijah | 59. Eliud |
| 14. Eber | 37. Asa | 60. Eleazar |
| 15. Peleg | 38. Jehoshaphat | 61. Matthan |
| 16. Reu | 39. Joram | 62. Jacob |
| 17. Serug | 40. Ahaziah | 63. Joseph |
| 18. Nahor | 41. Joash | 64. Jesus |
| 19. Terah | 42. Amaziah | |
| 20. Abraham | 43. Azzariah (Uzziah) | |
| 21. Isaac | 44. Jotham | |
| 22. Jacob | 45. Ahaz | |

*Name not reflected in Genesis or Chronicles genealogies, but recorded by Luke.

[Genealogy from "A Family Tree: from Adam to Jesus" copyright © 2014, Genesis Japan https://usstore.creation.com/genealogy-poster]

# CHAPTER 8

## DAILY READINGS
## AND
## INSIGHTS

# DAY 1

## WHAT'S THE MOST POPULAR VERSE IN THE BIBLE?

*[Scheduled Reading: Genesis 1-23]*

Greetings! For Day 1 reading, I have a question to consider.

**What's the most popular verse in the Bible?**

When I ask a room of children this question, everyone blurts out "John 3:16!" According to Google, they may be right.

Then I ask, "what's the most popular verse in the Old Testament?" I may hear Jeremiah 29:11... or Joshua 1:9...or Proverbs 3:5. Good guesses.

While not the most popular, one of the most <u>foundational</u> verses in the Old Testament is Genesis 3:15.

**And I will put enmity between you and the woman, and between your offspring and hers; he will crush your head, and you will strike his heel. (NIV)**

When God cursed the serpent after Adam and Eve had sinned, He delivered a verdict and a forecast of what was to come.

There's going to be a **Seed**—Jesus—who will come from the line of Eve. The serpent (Satan) will harass the earth and strike the heel of Jesus. In the end, Jesus will crush Satan's head.

Genesis 3:15 is arguably the most common stop-by verse for Bible theologians used to explain the Bible's systematic theology. From Genesis 3:15 forward, the rest of the Bible is all about working out this verse.

And sure enough, sixty-plus generations after Adam, this Holy

Spirit **"Seed"** is born – baby Jesus. Jesus grows up, walks the earth, dies a crucifixion death and miraculously rises again.

This resurrection event is a crushing blow to the serpent, but not the final blow. (Spoiler alert!) That comes in the book of Revelation.

**Genesis 3:15 is a mind-numbing prophecy and sums up the Bible narrative in less than 30 words.**

As you read today, and throughout these next 60 days, keep the big picture in mind.

Creation
Man's sin
Abraham & Sarah
Egypt is already a part of their lives
Abraham believed God
But Abraham & Sarah sinned
against God
God's covenant with Abraham

# DAY 2

## ADAM'S BIRTHDAY

*[Scheduled Reading: Genesis 24-39. Usually my comments will match up with the day's read. On rare occasion, it will not. That's the case for today while we're still building a big-picture foundation.]*

"When Adam had lived 130 years, he fathered a son in his own likeness, after his image, and named him Seth... When Seth had lived 105 years, he fathered Enosh... When Enosh had lived 90 years, he fathered Kenan..." (Genesis 5:3, 6, 9)

There's growing debate about the historical placement of Adam. How long ago was he on earth? Is Adam even real? Perhaps Adam and Eve are figurative characters?

Not in my Bible. I'm pretty much a literalist with the Bible. I take as much as I can at face value.

Why? Because of Chapters like **Genesis 5**. What appears to be a poetic rambling of "begats" (that's King James talk for "fathered") is actually the key to the historical dating of Adam.

From Adam to Noah are ten generations. A total of 1,656 years to the flood of Noah (go ahead, add them up).

It's this passage, along with the chronology in **Genesis 11** (and other passages), that helps us to date the approximate 4,000 years of Old Testament history.

**I have one simple question for us.** If Adam and Eve were not real characters, what's the point of passages like Genesis 5? Perhaps so we can have confidence in the dating of Biblical history.

**Can you believe we're almost through Genesis already?** I know, we just started! And that's how it is with the 60-day reading journey.

Jacob's name changed to Israel

Joseph sold into slavery by his brothers

# DAY 3

## GREAT, GREAT, GREAT, GREAT... GRANDFATHER

*[Scheduled Reading: Genesis 40 – Exodus 7]*

Have you ever wondered how many generations there are from Adam to Jesus Christ (aka *the Second Adam*)?

Approximately 64. That's right. It's not a thousand, or ten thousand, or a million.

As I shared yesterday, Genesis 5 gives us the ten generations from Adam to Noah. Genesis 11 gives us another ten generations to Abraham. And throughout the rest of the Bible you'll come across genealogy records charting the course of human history.

As we continue in our read, often it helps for me to ask myself, "Why is this story here?"

Often, it's simply because God is leaving us a trail of the family tree.

Like the bizarre story you just read in Genesis 38 of Judah, who went to a prostitute, who unbeknownst to him was his daughter-in-law, Tamar! (Yeah, crazy.) So why's that story there?

Maybe in keeping with God's pattern of tracking The Seed— the family tree from Adam to Christ. Jesus comes from Abraham, Isaac, Jacob, Judah... then baby Perez, the child of Tamar.

We'll encounter other stories along the way that are in the Bible simply to account for the genealogy of Jesus Christ.

There's a cool genealogy poster available at Creation Ministries International that I have found very helpful. It's an amazing collection of records from the Bible, and the mention of every single father in the line from Adam to Christ, and the applicable verse reference.

I highly recommend having this at home for further study and reference as you grow more familiar with the Bible. https://usstore.creation.com/genealogy-poster

Ok raft-mates, oars in the water. Time to paddle on.

(To follow the path of these 64 generations, see *Tracking "The Seed"* at *Chapter 7*)

In Chapter 42 referred to as Jacob
In chapter 43 referred to as Israel

Reuben, then Judah efforts to protect
Benjamin

Moses chosen to bring the people
out of Egypt.

# DAY 4

## KEY CONVERSATIONS

*[Scheduled Reading: Exodus 8-27. Notice today I introduce some **Speed 3** reading segments. That means, pick up the pace. This helps us to not get bogged down and to stay focused on the big picture.]*

In understanding the biblical narrative, there are **six conversations** that are considered "game changers" to working out God's plan.

Each of these conversations sets up a new chain of events that charts the course for The Seed, the offspring of the woman (Eve) we talked about on Day 1 in **Genesis 3:15**.

Four of these six conversations unfold in the first four days of the 60-day Bible read.

**Let's take a look:**

God curses the serpent (Satan). God sets in motion a new plan (Jesus will crush Satan) **[Genesis 3:15]**

God tells Noah to build an ark.God floods the earth and starts over with a new family **[Genesis 6-7]**

God covenants with Abraham that he will have a child. God births a new nation later called the Israelites **[Genesis 18 & 21]**

God commissions Moses to deliver the Israelites from slavery. God keeps the chosen nation alive and separated from pagan nations **[Exodus 3]**

The fifth and sixth events come later. God tells the prophet

Nathan that He will set up the future Kingdom through King David (5th conversation); an angel explains to Mary that she will have a child, conceived by the Holy Spirit (6th conversation). **This is Jesus, The Seed referenced back in Genesis 3:15**

We teach these events (often called "Bible stories") to children in Sunday school.

But often these kids grow up without understanding how they fit into the overall Biblical plan.

While reading the Bible, we can always keep this mega-theme in mind:

There's a battle going on between good and evil... between God and Satan. When Satan makes a move, God responds.

- Satan tempts Eve (and Adam) to sin; God issues a curse...and a plan.
- Satan perpetuates evil on earth; God responds with a flood.
- Satan revives wickedness and rebellion; God selects a father (Abraham) of a chosen nation to carry The Seed forward.
- Satan works to drive Israelites into slavery and submission to the Egyptians; God uses Moses to break them free.
- Rebellion sets in again and the twelve tribes of Israel are eventually exiled; In due time, God inserts this Holy Spirit Seed inside the virgin Mary and Jesus is born.

**Tomorrow we'll put these pieces together in a memorable way.**

# DAY 5

## THE BIBLE'S BIG PICTURE

*[Scheduled Reading: Exodus 28-Leviticus 7]*

When I teach the Bible narrative to families, here's what I tell them.

The Bible is about the journey of The Seed that travels through:

> ➤ **4,000** years (see Day 2), consisting of roughly
> ➤ **sixty-four (64)** generations (see Day 3), connected by
> ➤ **six (6)** key conversations (Day 4), focused on
> ➤ **two (2)** resurrection events, which set up
> ➤ **one (1)** final climactic, redemptive event... the recreation of the heavens and earth.

**For the past five days, we've been unpacking this story... piece by piece.**

Having this narrative in mind will help us throughout the rest of our Bible read.

OK, we're in Leviticus now. And that means... read quickly.

(See Chapter 7 for a view of *The Bible's Big Picture Timeline*)

# DAY 6

## SERIOUS BUSINESS

*[Scheduled Reading: Leviticus 8-27. Mostly "Speed 3" reading.]*

I was cruising along at high reading speed (that's what you do in Leviticus) when I came across the sad story in chapter 24... the story of the boy who cursed a blasphemy against God.

The people brought him before Moses and they waited on the Lord. Finally God's verdict arrived. "Stone him."

So that's what the people did.

**There must be more to blasphemy than we can comprehend.**

If there's a transgression that should haunt us, it's when we hear God's name used in vain. But we hear it every day, all the time.

Often there's little we can do about it – like when you're at work listening to your boss... or when kids hear it in the hallways at school.

But sometimes it's a choice. Like with just about every TV sitcom or box office movie.

My father has a strong filter for blasphemy. In my youth if we were watching TV or a movie as a family, and if God's name was used flippantly in any way, the TV went off.

We might have been settling into the story and really enjoying the show – but it didn't matter. There were no warnings or second chances for the TV program. Just the click of the remote.

As I grew older, I came to appreciate Dad's actions.

Hearing God's name in vain should bother us – like nails on the chalkboard. We should cringe at the hearing of such talk and do what we can to shut it down.

I understand "not offending others" or forcing my faith on those who don't know better. So when I hear it used in public, there's very little to do about it.

But when it's just my wife, children and me enjoying a family movie night at home, and the blasphemy starts swinging, I have a choice.

Thanks to that unfortunate story in Leviticus, and my father's example, I'm reminded the right choice is to hit the remote (OFF).

There must be more to blasphemy than we can comprehend. But we can comprehend that it's dangerous.

# DAY 7

## FLYING HIGH

*[Scheduled Reading: Numbers 1-17]*

**We're flying through the Bible, aren't we!**

In a few days we will have covered the first five books (called the Torah.) Some of this content is Speed 2 & 3 material. It's easy to get bogged down in these areas, but we want to keep moving.

**So what's going on in Exodus, Leviticus, Numbers & Deuteronomy?**

God's working a plan to route The Seed through the nation of Israel (the twelve tribes of Jacob). From the time of Moses, it will be roughly 1,500 years into the future until this eventual seed (Jesus) takes its place on the cross.

**So while Satan is working feverishly to destroy the "seed" carriers (Israelites), God is building them for survival.**

This Israelite nation must be strong, independent, well financed, heavily armed. And they need a government that can sustain order. (Think about the U.S. We need those things, too.)

**To set up this sustaining government, God gives them several things (all "L's"):**

- **Label** - He called them Israelites. He also called Israel His "firstborn son." Extremely symbolic isn't it? Don't lose sight of this idea.

- **Land** - That's the Promise Land! They wandered in the wilderness for forty years to get in. Once they finally entered, they set up permanent residence. The twelve tribes were counted in a census, and given their respective land allotments (read Numbers).

- **Location (of worship)** - While the Israelites wandered for forty years, whenever they stopped to set up camp...the tabernacle went up. And that's where they worshipped. Much detail Bible text is committed to this elaborate tent design and related worship practices.

- **Laws** - God installed a system of sacrifices and laws to remind them of God's holiness...of their sin...and of the way things ought to be had man never sinned. So if a young man skinned his knee on a rock and suffered an open cut wound while playing with his kids, he was considered "unclean." In this case, the man didn't do anything wrong. God just wanted them to understand, "it wasn't intended to be this way" (skinning knees, that is). These laws were very detailed and often confusing...and sometimes weird. And yes, lots of redundancy.

- **Leader** - Yeah, that would be Moses. And eventually Joshua.

- **Levites** - This tribe was set apart to run the government, sort of like our congress (without the entertaining election cycles). They managed the tabernacle, administered laws, performed sacrifices, etc. Their work was funded by an elaborate system of gifts and offerings from the other tribes.

Throughout the rest of the Old Testament, we'll see this system at work. It functioned on occasion, but broke down most of the time.

**Still God's primary purpose was intact. Keeping the nation of Israel alive... which meant keeping The Seed alive.**

Okay, time to get some altitude... back to reading.

# DAY 8

## GOD'S RULES

*[Scheduled Reading: Numbers 18-36]*

In the past few years, I became a college wrestling fan. Before I understood the rules, the sport seemed goofy and strange. Men grabbing men in uncomfortable ways, in weird positions and angles.

But now that I know the rules, a good match can put me at the edge of my seats.

The Bible is that way. If you don't know the rules, the Bible can seem odd. **But if you understand God's rules, it makes more sense.**

In context of the Bible, we call these rules "doctrines."

A doctrine is a code of beliefs that represents what we believe about the Bible. Because the word "doctrine" can sound intimidating, or even boring, I like to call them "God's rules" (that gets my attention).

Here are some of GOD's Rules, from God's perspective.

1. I AM WHO I AM! [This is a big one… self-explanatory. God is God. He sets the standard for all things: for time, space, holiness, etc.]

   a. Doctrine of God.

2. I can take what was once made perfect by my hands, allow it be become imperfect… then make it perfect again. [Do you ever wonder why God allowed sin and evil? At some point, we must get over it. He allowed it and He's working it out. It's one of God's rules.]

a. Doctrine of redemption

b. Doctrine of heaven

c. Doctrine of salvation

3. I can take what was once made perfect, allow it to become imperfect... and let it stay that way forever. [BOOM. We take this idea for granted... but it's stunning when you think about it.]

    a. Doctrines of sin, death, Satan, demons

    b. Doctrines of hell, judgments

    (Great White Throne Judgment)

4. I'm a very creative and symbolic God. Some of my creativity I share with creation. Some of it is so cryptic man will never figure it out. (One of many aspects of God)

5. One of my favorite tools for symbolism is blood (sacrifices, covenants, etc.) [Why blood? I, Jeff, have no idea. God could have used anything. This is one of those rules we must accept, and appreciate.]

6. In order to atone for sin, something had to die. [Again, why death? It's God's Rules... that's why.)

    a. Doctrines of sin, atonement, sanctification

7. I can plant a human seed in a mother's womb, to be given birth as a newborn baby, grow up as a child, experience adulthood as a man and have the power and mind of God. [Mind-numbing idea. We must not grow casual with this awesome rule]

    a. Doctrine of the trinity

    b. Doctrine of the virgin birth

## It's not our job to fully comprehend all the rules.

But it helps to know them so we can connect the dots in understanding scripture. By knowing God's rules and accepting the terms, we can make the Bible less complicated, and even wildly interesting. And of course, come to saving faith in Christ.

# DAY 9

## PAY ATTENTION, PARENTS

*[Scheduled Reading: Deuteronomy 1-15]*

**For parents with children at home, today's reading offers us a special challenge.**

The words of Deuteronomy were delivered by Moses at the very end of a 40-year season of wilderness-craziness - just before the Israelites enter the promised land.

**Moses reminds the Israelites to teach God's Words to their children.** It's almost as if he knew they wouldn't (he knew them well) and that particular disasters would follow if they took their eyes off God and His Word.

If there's one theme that repeats throughout the Old Testament, it's how mankind continues to fall back in touch with their rebellious nature. No matter how miraculous God's rescue and deliverance is, and how genuine the people's response of repentance and forgiveness, God's children seem to drift again... and again.

Pay attention to Moses' charge to parents in Deuteronomy, Chapters 4, 6 and 11. Here's the one in chapter 6.

**"Hear, O Israel: The Lord our God, the Lord is one. You shall love the Lord your God with all your heart and with all your soul and with all your might. And these words that I command you today shall be on your heart.**

**You shall teach them diligently to your children, and shall talk of them when you sit in your house, and when you walk by the way, and when you lie down, and when you rise." —
Deuteronomy 6:4-7**

(Tough to do this without reading His Word ourselves, right?)

# DAY 10

## CONGRATULATIONS

*[Scheduled Reading: Deuteronomy 16-34]*

**Today, I just want to say... Congratulations!**

**You're at Day 10 (smiles).**

After today's reading you'll be through what's called the Pentateuch, the first five books of the Bible (and what the Jews call the Torah.)

In ten more days, you'll be reading in Chronicles. And at Day 30, you'll be finishing Psalms.

That's pretty cool isn't it?! I think so.

I hope you're having a positive experience in God's Word.

**The next several days will bring some great stories - Joshua, Judges, Ruth, 1 Samuel - and some smoother tracks for reading.**

# DAY 11

## MINI MO

*[Scheduled Reading: Joshua 1-21]*

**Joshua was a cool cat. Sort of a cross between Moses and King David.**

I heard a Bible teacher once refer to Joshua as "Mini Mo" (for little Moses). Joshua was successor to Moses and took the Israelites into the promised land. He was also a fierce warrior - like King David who came along later.

**One of the most effective leadership transitions in the Old Testament has to be the one between Moses and Joshua.** Maybe because both men understood the importance of God's Word.

You just read in **Deuteronomy 31**, where Moses commissioned Joshua and instructed the Israelites to read the entire law publicly at the end of every seven years (verse 10-13).

Sure enough, some time later Joshua read the entire law to a public assembly, including *the women, and the little ones, and the sojourners* (Joshua 8:35).

**Joshua was very mindful to make sure the people passed the knowledge of God to the next generation (Joshua 4:6,21).**

Near the end of his lifetime, Joshua made his famous public stand: *as for me and my house, we will serve the Lord.* (24:15).

Then something interesting happens.

Joshua *wrote these words in the Books of the Law of God*

(24:26). And what words might these be? The very words we're reading in Joshua. It's his book. His writing became part of the canonized scriptures we're reading today.

Very few Old Testament leaders share the legacy of Joshua. Scriptures say *Israel served the Lord all the days of Joshua, and all the days of the elders who out-lived Joshua and had known all the work that the Lord did for Israel* (24:31).

**I'm inspired to be like Mini Mo.**

To treasure God's Word. To read it publicly in my home. And to pass down the knowledge of God to the next generation in my home.

# DAY 12

## WHY ALL THE BLOODSHED?

*[Scheduled Reading: Joshua 22-24; Judges 1-15]*

**Often reading through the Old Testament feels like an endless list of casualty records—like reading about America's Civil War, only much worse.**

Lot's of killing. Big battles. Non-stop bloodshed.

What's the reason for all this death? Why was God so set on helping the Israelites to wipe out their enemies? And why, all of the sudden, does the killing campaign end as we enter the New Testament? Why the shift in strategy from destruction of enemies to "turning the other cheek"?

### It's all about The Seed

Again, for 4,000 years God is working The Seed through history. Preserving the path for The Seed involves survival—keeping the lineage of Israel alive. And this means destroying enemies that stand in the way.

Time and time again, God's supernatural intervention leads to massive death and destruction of humans. It's hard for us to relate to this today. But it's a testament to how God has preserved The Seed over the course of history.

As The Seed gets closer to the New Testament, the killing campaigns end. God even allows Israel to be exiled. But He keeps The Seed alive.

Once Jesus Christ finally appears on the scene, the campaign of destruction is replaced with a campaign of deliverance. Instead of destroying enemies that stand in the way, these enemies have the opportunity to be delivered from the wrath of sin.

# DAY 13

## CONNECTING THE DOTS

*[Scheduled Reading: Judges 16-21; Ruth; 1 Samuel 1-10]*

***Am I not a Benjaminite, from the least of the tribes of Israel? And is not my clan the humblest of all the clans of the tribe of Benjamin?*** (1 Samuel 9:21)

One of the cool things about reading 15-20 chapters a day is the opportunity to connect the dots.

In today's scheduled read, you'll see in Judges 20 about Israel's war with one of their tribesmen – the Benjaminites.

It was a nasty fight that follows a most gruesome story about a Levite who cut up his dead concubine into 12 pieces and sent her throughout all the territory of Israel. (The Levite's concubine had been murdered by some Benjaminites in an all-night rape.)

**This was before Wiki-leaks and fake news, but I'm sure rumors were still strong.**

When folks learned this event wasn't fake news, it got all of them fired up... against the Benjaminites.

400,000 Israelites (from the 11 tribes) took on 26,000 Benjaminites. It was a blood-bath. Over 25,000 Benjaminite men were lost at battle, leaving 600 men running for the hills. The tribe was nearly wiped out.

It was a sad day for Israel.

**Now let's connect some dots that all occur in this one day's reading:**

1.  Fast forward through Ruth and into 1 Samuel, Saul is being picked as Israel's new king. Saul says to Samuel, *Am I not a Benjaminite, from the least of the tribes of Israel? And is not my clan the humblest of all the clans of the tribe of Benjamin?*

This makes more sense as to what Saul meant: ***What kind of stigma must it have been for Saul to grow up a Benjaminite?***

2.  Another thought nugget is when Saul is introduced as the son of Kish, a "Benjaminite, a man of wealth" (1 Samuel 9:1). It makes sense this man Kish was a wealth-holder given that his ancestors were among the few survivors of the Benjaminite blood bath. These survivors likely inherited some of the land previously owned by their Benjaminite brothers.
3.  In the next day's reading (1 Samuel), David appears. Where does David come from? The tribe of Judah, the son of Jesse, the son of Obed. Where does Obed come from? From Ruth, the Moabite who married Boaz. (The book of Ruth is sandwiched between Judges and 1 Samuel).

These are quite a few interesting connections in just a few day's reading. **Enjoy today's read. Keep the pace.**

# DAY 14

## WHEN THE BIBLE SHOUTS

*[Scheduled Reading: 1 Samuel 11-27]*

Another cool thing happens when power-reading through the Bible.

**Mega-themes shout for your attention.**

Like this theme from Samuel's farewell address: ***Do not turn aside from following the Lord, but serve the Lord with all your heart*** (1 Samuel 12:20).

Then again a few verses later, ***Only fear the Lord and serve him faithfully with all your heart*** (v24).

Who does that sound like? It sounds like Joshua before him...and Moses before Joshua.

Like a bull-horn message from a burdened prophet, we are reminded of this theme over and over again - all throughout Exodus, Numbers, Deuteronomy, Joshua, Judges.... and now Samuel.

**Serve the Lord with all your heart... do not turn away from serving the Lord.**

Keep reading, my friends. Listen to the whispers... and the screams.

# DAY 15

## BIG

*[Scheduled Reading: 1 Samuel 28 - 2 Samuel 15]*

**Everything about David's life was BIG.**

His dreams were BIG.

The giant he faced was BIG.

The battles he fought were BIG.

His fame was BIG. His enemies were BIG.

The sin he committed was BIG.

The fallout from his sin was BIG.

His vision to build God a house was BIG.

His family was BIG.

His bodyguards were BIG.

His sacrifices were BIG.

His praises were BIG (wait till you read Psalms :)

When reading about King David, it's hard to not fall into a trance and feel like the stories you're reading are the make-believe kind. But they're not. They happened.

**Something else was BIG. God's covenant with David. God promised to establish David's throne FOREVER** (2 Samuel 7:16). That's BIG!

I'm not sure what David thought of this promise. Does anything on earth last forever? Kingdoms rise and kingdoms fall. But forever is exactly what God had in mind.

To fast forward, Jesus is the King that comes in the line of David. And Christ will stand on the throne FOREVER.

Throughout the rest of the Bible-read, you'll see mention of names like Abraham, Judah... and David.

These men fall in the line of The Seed mentioned in Genesis 3:15. **Like the founding father faces on Mount Rushmore, King David's name is frequently connected to the coming messiah.**

That's BIG.

# DAY 16

## MORE BIG

*[Scheduled Reading: 2 Samuel 16-24; 1 Kings 1-5]*

**King David's BIG legacy continues through his son Solomon.**

David must have taught his son to think BIG. And more importantly, to pray BIG (1 Kings 3).

In response to a BIG dream, a BIG offer, and a BIG ask, God gives Solomon wisdom and wealth in unprecedented proportions.

**But something sad is about to happen in tomorrow's read. A BIG fall.**

Solomon turns away from God. As BIG as David's story was, Solomon's fall is equally devastating. Tragic.

**After reaching its peak, Israel's decline sets in and never fully recovers. The rest of the Old Testament is about Israel's decline and desolation.**

But God leaves a flickering light for a very small recovery. Just enough to keep His BIG covenant with King David... and to keep The Seed alive.

# DAY 17

## SPEED BUMPS AHEAD!

*[Scheduled Reading: 1 Kings 6-20]*

**I want to call attention to a speed bump in today's reading: 1 Kings 11 & 12.**

It's a sad few chapters, actually.

**God is preparing to break up Israel on account of Solomon's fade from God. Israel will split into ten northern tribes (called Israel in Samaria) and two southern tribes (called Judah in Jerusalem).**

It doesn't help that the two initial leaders are named Jeroboam (Israel's king) and Rehoboam (Judah's king). That's one of the challenges of Bible reading - all the names start to run together.

Throughout the rest of Kings and then 2 Chronicles, the authors bounce back and forth between the accounts of kings in Judah and Israel.

In my past Bible read-through attempts, I missed these speed bump moments and it sure made reading difficult for me in the sections ahead.

**It's important to remember that Judah is the line that God will use to work The Seed from Genesis 3:15 (that ultimately arrives to Mary and Joseph).**

OK, carry on. There are some Speed 2/3 zones ahead, and I just wanted to make sure you caught this critical historical tidbit in 1 Kings 11 & 12.

# DAY 18

## SEE THE BIG PICTURE

*[Scheduled Reading: 1 Kings 21-22; 2 Kings 1-14]*

**Some reading segments are harder than others. Today's read can be difficult. Maybe even like reading Leviticus!**

Bouncing around from king to king (mostly bad ones), and back and forth between Judah and Israel, tripping over difficult-to-remember names and depressing themes. Focus is hard.

**These were dark times for Israel. Famine, constant war, wickedness. In 2 Kings, we have:**

> ➤ Two starving mothers forced to cook their sons to eat (Ch. 6)
> ➤ Jezebel thrown from a tower and devoured by dogs (Ch. 9)
> ➤ A king's mother kills the entire royal family - except for a child who escapes (Ch. 11)
> ➤ Even the somewhat good kings had dark tasks to perform – Jehu invites 80 prophets of Baal to a worship gathering so he can have them slaughtered (Ch. 10)
> ➤ And some weird stuff, too – a dead man touches the bones of Elisha and is resurrected (Ch. 13)

**With an eye on the big picture, here's what's happening...**

Solomon's fade from God set in motion a downward spiral for both of the resulting kingdoms, Judah and Israel. Both are headed toward captivity and we're in the final stretch.

Hang on readers...

# DAY 19

## DARKNESS

*[Scheduled Reading: 2 Kings 15-25; 1 Chronicles 1-5]*

**Darkness is still the big theme.** One of Judah's kings (Ahaz) burns his own son as an offering (2 Kings 16). UNTHINKABLE!

How does humanity sink so low? And we're talking about descendants of King David!

**This brings us to the exile of both Israel (northern kingdom falls, Chapter 17) and Judah (southern kingdom falls, Chapter 25).**

What's so amazing to me is the erratic see-sawing of good kings and bad kings. After the horrible child-sacrificing Ahaz, Judah has a very good king, Hezekiah.

(Think about it, Hezekiah's brother was sacrificed by their father Ahaz).

Following Hezekiah is a horrible King Manasseh (who also burned his son as an offering). After one more wicked son-king (Amon), Judah has one of its legendary God-fearing kings (Josiah).

Josiah discovers the book of the law and restores the laws, the feasts and sacrifices.

And as the see-saw pattern continues to play out, the next kings are wicked again... and finally Jerusalem is captured by Babylon (Chapter 25).

**It's a dark chapter for the fate of The Seed. But God keeps a remnant alive and the rest of the story is ahead of us.**

# DAY 20

## REFRESHER TIME

*[Scheduled Reading: 1 Chronicles 6-23]*

After a genealogy review, we're back into the accounts of King David. In Bible reading, I always welcome the chance to revisit previous time periods (I need the refresher).

**1 Chronicles covers the same events of 2 Samuel, but gives greater attention to King David.**

Remember, everything about David was BIG. His entourage, his military, and size of government. His three mighty men were impressive.

And the 30 were like his secret service – but more like Rambo characters. He had over 1 million warriors. There were 38,000 Levites (think of congress - their functions, not their size :) And 4,000 of them were dedicated to music – that's some choir to offer fitting praises to the Lord.

For the reader, on one hand it's raw data... not so exciting. On the other hand, **putting this data in context helps to appreciate what kind of kingdom David had.** Yes, BIG. Impressive.

The other theme that jumped out to me in today's reading is how serious God treated sin (1 Chron 21.)

David's sin of ordering the census cost the lives of 70,000 men. God was actually prepared to wipe out all of Jerusalem (UNBELIEVABLE), but then changed his mind and stopped the angel from further destruction (v15).

This happened before... when God wanted to wipe out the Israelites when Moses was receiving the Ten Commandments, but Moses pleaded for, and received, God's mercy.

# DAY 21

## REPETITION AND REPETITION

*[Scheduled Reading: 1 Chronicles 24-29; 2 Chronicles 1-16]*

**Seeing double?**

**What's the point of all this repetition?**

2 Chronicles is a rehash of 1 & 2 Kings. Just look at it like the four gospel accounts, each covering the life of Christ, but from the perspective of a different author.

It makes sense that the Bible would give special real estate to the kingdoms of David and Solomon. These were the times Israel was functioning at its greatest capacity. Manpower was massive (remember all the details of King David's BIG armies, singers, Levites, etc.). And wealth was enormous, especially under King Solomon.

And for a season, worship to God was clicking.

**Much of the Old Testament is either about, or authored by, David and Solomon.**

In addition to their accounts in Samuel, Chronicles, and Kings, together these two men are responsible for much of the Psalms, and all of Proverbs, Ecclesiastes and Songs of Solomon.

**David and Solomon's reign marks Israel's greatest strength and prosperity.... EVER. From there, it's all downhill.**

# DAY 22

## NEVER IN A HURRY

*[Scheduled Reading: 2 Chronicles 17-35]*

When you're doing a 60-day Bible read and trekking through the Old Testament, reading assignments start crisscrossing.

You start a particular day's reading and the story sounds familiar. *Didn't I just read this story yesterday?*

That's what happens in 2 Chronicles. The book retraces the events of 1 & 2 Kings - another walk through the good and bad kings. Once again, after Solomon the kingdoms split between Judah (two southern tribes) and Israel (ten northern tribes).

For the rest of the book, the author seems to focus primarily on the kings of Judah (and not so much Israel).

I've marked this section as Speed 2 or 3 reading (your pick).

**You might slow down for the accounts of Hezekiah (chapters 29-32) and Josiah (chapters 34-35).**

More real estate has been given to these two favorable kings – both undertook considerable efforts to restore old customs from the Law.

What's disturbing is how there never seems to be two good kings in a row. Shocking, really.

We're now done with the era of kings as both Israel and Judah are exiled. Babylonian rule takes over next... for 70 years.

**Stepping back to the big picture...**

God is taking His time, working The Seed through the line of

King David. Each of Judah's kings, good ones and bad, are passing along The Seed of Eve that will eventually work it's way to Mary and Joseph, the parents of Jesus Christ.

He's never in a hurry. But we are. Back to reading!

# DAY 23

## TURNING POINT

*[Scheduled Reading: 2 Chronicles 36, Ezra, Nehemiah 1-7]*

**The books Ezra and Nehemiah are significant turning points for the story of Israel.**

After a 70-year exile, God opens the door for a return to Jerusalem. Notice the language in Ezra 1:1 (and again in Chapter 6) of how God uses other leaders, like Cyrus king of Persia, to give a new birth for the Israelite nation. There's a mega-theme for us here - GOD GETS HIS WAY... ALWAYS!

Through the leadership of Ezra, the people return to rebuild the temple. And through Nehemiah, they rebuild the wall. Together they help to restore working order for Judah.

**And guess who happens to be among the named exiles who returns to Jerusalem in Ezra 2:2?**

Zerubbabel!

**"And who is Zerubbabel?" you ask.**

He's a descendant of David - and the one who will carry The Seed forward. (You'll find his name sprinkled nine times throughout Ezra and Nehemiah. Can you find them :)

**And guess who surfaces exactly ten more generations into the future from Zerubbabel?**

Joseph, the carpenter... the father of Jesus.

The big picture is coming into view.

# DAY 24

## THE JEWISH TRIFECTA

*[Scheduled Reading: Nehemiah 8-13, Esther, Job 1-8]*

**When we hear of the Holocaust, we think of six million Jews killed by Hitler in the 1940's. We forget sometimes that Jewish genocide has been ongoing for the past 3,500 years.**

Pharoah set out to kill baby boys because the Jewish race was growing too quickly. (Remember Moses in the basket?)

King Herod set out to destroy baby boys as well (Mary and Joseph escaped to Egypt with baby Jesus).

**The story of Esther is yet another example of an attempt to exterminate the Jews.**

The reversal of fate on Haman is one of the most entertaining plot twists in all of scriptures. Read this book leisurely - and enjoy its drama.

Once again, God delivers the Jews from extinction.

Ezra-Nehamiah-Esther can be considered the Jewish-trifecta in keeping The Seed alive with a remaining remnant of Israel.

# DAY 25

## JOB

*[Scheduled Reading: Job 9-34]*

Job has always been one of my favorite Bible characters.

I've read the book many times in my life. Job is one of God's superstars. I've always wanted to be a man like Job, one that God might boast about (just not in front of Satan).

Job is the first book in the series of what's called the "wisdom literature" section of the Bible - with Psalm, Proverbs, Ecclesiastes, and Songs.

Did you know Job is the oldest book in the Bible? It is believed this account occurred approximately 100 years before Abraham.

Unfortunately, some misinformed teachers have even questioned whether Job is a real character or just a fictitious one.

But I have a clue to share that proves Job's life story is the real deal. I'll save that nugget for later.

# Day 26

## CATCH-UP TIME

*[Scheduled Reading: Job 35-42, Psalm 1-24]*

**You'll notice I graded some of the wisdom books (Job, Psalm, Proverbs) as Speed 1, 2, or 3. That means, your choice.**

It can be a chance to catch-up with the plan if you need. Just fly through the pages.

It can be hard to get much out of these poetic texts during a power read pace during the 60-day read. In reality, these poetic texts are designed for deep reflection and meditation.

When reading through the Psalms during the 60-day read, sometimes I will start with a few chapters and digest slowly. Then after what might seem like a short quiet time session, I'll pick up the pace.

**Bottom line - move quickly.**

As always - this is your plan. Make it fit you. For me, it's a chance to give my brain a break as I head toward Day 30, the midway point.

# DAY 27

## INTERESTING MAN

*[Scheduled Reading: Psalm 25-54]*

**David was an interesting man.**

A song writer like Steven Curtis Chapman. A fierce warrior like William Wallace (Braveheart). A man after God's heart, like Billy Graham... or Eugene Peterson.

It is believed that nearly half (73) of the 150 psalms were written by King David.

When you think of today's budding music stars on The Voice, or American Idol, think of the talented young man David, chosen by King Saul to play the harp for him in his house. He likely built on his craft as a musician during those days.

But perhaps his real music launch occurred while tending his father's sheep, out in the fields all alone with God. The psalms show how David poured his heart out to God. Which brings up a few questions.

**How do you share your heart with God?**

Do you journal your thoughts, prayers, praises to God? Do you take prayer walks?

**As you think about David's walk with God, think about what your walk with God looks like... from God's perspective.**

# DAY 28

## PRAYER JOURNAL

*[Scheduled Reading: Psalm 55-84]*

**I started journaling prayers to God over two decades ago.**

I was in a career transition having had just started my own business. It was a very volatile and emotional venture (as a stock daytrader) and I was dependant on God for success... and sanity. I was 27 years old and my faith journey was starting to sprout.

I didn't realize it at the time, but looking back I now see clear connection between my early seasons of journaling and growth in my faith.

One of the great benefits of journaling is being able to go back and review various stages of my life.

**I can see how God carried me through seasons of trials and triumphs, joys and disappointments. I can see repeated themes that help me understand Jeff... and better understand God.**

Most importantly, I see the proof and faithfulness of God's attention to my life. That's comforting.

I don't journal every day. Sometimes I go weeks or months without journaling. Still I have filled several notebooks over the years of my thoughts, prayers and discussions with God.

**Keep in mind that as you read through the Psalms, you're reading through someone's prayer journal. Pretty cool.**

# DAY 29

## MUSIC IN CHURCH

*[Scheduled Reading: Psalm 85-115]*

**Who are the sons of Korah? (Psalm 85, 87, 88...) And what about Asaph? (Psalm 80, 81, 82, 83, etc.)**

Remember the 4,000 musicians King David organized in 1 Chronicles 23?

Well, Asaph ( 1 Chron. 15:19, 16:5) and Korah (2 Chron 20:19) are among the many songwriters and music directors mentioned at various times in Chronicles.

In fact, the sons of Asaph are referenced in Ezra and Nehemiah, continuing to live out the family legacy as song and worship leaders.

Vocal and instrumental music worship continues to play a significant role throughout the Old Testament. And wait until we get to Revelation - 100 million angels singing praises to the Lamb.

**Back to those 4,000 singers David organized. I wonder if music style and preferences ever became an issue like it can be in churches today?**

Okay... Back to reading.

# DAY 30

## PSALM 119 IS A TREASURE

*[Scheduled Reading: Psalm 116-150]*

Be sure to take note of Psalm 119 (*You won't miss it - Ha!*).

**It's the longest Psalm, and the longest chapter in the Bible. Would you believe that it has more verses (176) than 21 of the books of the Bible?! No kidding.**

This psalm is organized around 22 stanzas, one for each letter of the Hebrew alphabet.

Each verse contains a word or phrase that refers to God's Word: i.e. "laws", "commandments", "statutes", "ways", "testimonies", "precepts", etc.

One season, I was feeling flat in my Bible engagement and seeking greater traction in my Bible reading. It was before I did my first power-read through scriptures.

I found great encouragement and inspiration from this chapter, taking the time to highlight every single mention of reference to God's Word.

**This is definitely a chapter to return to after you complete the 60-day Bible read, to spend time reading slowly and deeply.**

Psalm 119 is a treasure.

# DAY 31

## HALFTIME

*[Scheduled Reading: Proverbs 1-19]*

**Today is the beginning of the second half. You've read thru half the Bible in 30 days. That's pretty cool.**

We're now digging into Solomon's writings. It's hard to believe that for a man who shipwrecked his faith late in life, so many precious texts are attributed to him.

It's ironic that one of the snares Solomon speaks to - the adulteress - was the very snare that trapped Solomon.

Actually it may not have been adultery that snared Solomon. (How does a man with 1,000 wives and concubines commit adultery?!) More specifically, it was that Solomon married foreign wives and they turned his heart to their foreign gods.

Not wise.

Still, Solomon's timeless proverbs holds true. Somehow Solomon's son, Rehoboam, missed these gems.

# DAY 32

## MEANINGLESS, MEANINGLESS

*[Schedule Reading: Proverbs 20-31, Ecclesiastes 1-8]*

Ecclesiastes is another one of my favorite books. It's a fascinating perspective from history's wisest person.

I like the theme (everything is meaningless). Really, I'm not a depressing person, but this book can seem that way to some. (Although I have always preferred cloudy, rainy days over sunshine and I'm not sure why.)

Mainly, I like the simplicity of which Solomon speaks.

**The more wisdom, the more grief.**

**The more you accomplish, the less significant it seems.**

**Our job is really simple; enjoy your work and sleep good at night.**

**Things in life don't always make sense.**

**One thing that should makes sense — to fear God.**

I especially like the last two verses of the book (tomorrow's scheduled read):

> *Now all has been heard; here is the conclusion of the matter. Fear God and keep his commandments, for this is the whole duty of man. For God will bring every deed into judgment, including every hidden thing, whether it is good or evil.*

> (Eccl. 12:13-14).

I actually created a song on this passage for my kids when they were young. (Sorry, I won't sing it for you.)

# DAY 33

## TRANSITION TIME

*[Scheduled Reading: Ecclesiastes 9-12, Songs, Isaiah 1-9]*

**We're coming out of the wisdom literature and heading into the prophets. I'll have more to say about prophet-reading tomorrow.**

But first, some basics:

> ➤ There are 17 books in the "prophet" section
> ➤ The first 5 are considered the "major prophets;" the next 12, "minor prophets"
> ➤ The 5 major prophets cover nearly 200 pages in my Bible (1,042 pages); the minor prophets cover just 50 pages
> ➤ Most of the prophet periods occurred before Israel and Judah's captivity; but a few (i.e. Malachi, Haggai, Zechariah) occurred after their captivity
> ➤ Most of the prophets came out of the southern kingdom (Judah) but a few (i.e. Jonah, Hosea) out of northern tribes (Israel)

It doesn't help that these prophet books are not chronological.

They bounce around from era to era and back and forth between Judah and Israel. At least the last three books of the Old Testament - Haggai, Zechariah, Malachi - finish out chronologically.

**Initially for me, the prophets were among the toughest sections of the scriptures to read. But over time, as my Bible knowledge grew my appreciation of the prophets did, too.**

For our 60-day plan, I've marked the five Major Prophets with lots of Speed 2 reading. But if you want to power faster at Speed 3 pace, go for it.

# DAY 34

## HITTING THE WALL

*[Schedule Reading: Isaiah 10-31]*

**Marathon runners (which I am not) know about hitting "the wall."**

The wall is that point in the run when your body cramps up, your legs feel like jelly, and your head teases you with ideas like pulling to the edge of the cement for a nap.

I'm told the familiar place to find the wall is around mile 20, six miles short of finish. It's past the midpoint, but still a ways to go.

**For 60-day Bible readers, you could call the Major Prophets "the wall."**

For the next ten days, we'll be slogging through five books. Really, it's the big three - Isaiah, Jeremiah and Ezekiel - that are the most difficult for me, because they're really long.

These books are fascinating and there's no need to fear them. But for power reading, it is challenging.

**If this is your first fast paced Bible read, I don't want you to hit the wall. Do whatever you need to get through it. Because when you come out of it, you'll be on the homestretch.**

The minor prophets will be sprints... and you'll be shocked how quickly we'll breeze through the New Testament.

Read along, friends. Don't slow down.

# DAY 35

## A VOICE IN THE WILDERNESS

*[Schedule Reading: Isaiah 32-47]*

**A voice cries: 'in the wilderness prepare the way of the Lord; make straight in the desert a highway for our God' (Isaiah 40:3).**

I suspect that 2,000 years ago, when the little Jewish boys and girls were learning to read from the scrolls, they all learned Isaiah 40:3.

I imagine they memorized it in "Scroll Class," like kids today recite John 3:16 in Sunday school.

Of course, the gospel accounts had not yet been written - so the prophet scrolls would have been the most fresh texts available.

**It is interesting that all four of the gospel writers - Matthew, Mark, Luke and John - quote Isaiah 40:3 early in their accounts.**

That voice "in the wilderness" is that of John the Baptist... the prophet of prophets. John was the prophet of whom the historic prophet Isaiah spoke, the one who would come to prepare the way for the messiah.

The Jews were eager for this future prophet to arrive.

Consider the attention the future antichrist receives today? *Who will he be? From where will he arrive? And when will he arrive?*

Being a prophet of light, John's arrival must certainly have been eagerly awaited. After Israel's downfall, exile and eventual return to their land, the future hope for the Jews was to be ushered in by this prophet character.

**While not everyone was paying attention, many were. Especially those who read and studied the prophets.**

# Day 36

## ARE YOU CONNECTING THE DOTS?

*[Scheduled Reading: Isaiah 48-66]*

I'm beginning to see why Bible students love the prophets.

Are you?

They're loaded with connect-the-dot moments.

**Reading the prophets can be like searching for seashells on the beach. There's LOTS of them. And just when you find a pretty one, there's another... and then another... and another...**

Let's marvel at a few of them:

> ➤ Isaiah 53 - references to Christ, the coming Messiah, all throughout this chapter

> ➤ Isaiah 59:17 - you wonder where Apostle Paul got some of his teaching material for the "armor of God" teaching at Ephesians 6:13-17?

> ➤ Isaiah 60:11,19,20 - references to heaven also at Revelation 21

> ➤ Isaiah 65:17-25 - weaves in and out of references to the new heavens, new earth

> ➤ Isaiah 61:1, 2 - the very passage Jesus quotes when he stands in the temple to read from the scroll of the prophet Isaiah (Luke 4:17-19) - very cool!

> ➤ Isaiah 66:1,2 - the passage Stephen quotes from his speech just before he is being stoned (in Acts 7:49,50)

**Once again, before the New Testament books were written, what were the New Testament writers and characters reading?**

Answer: the prophets.

Congratulations. You've now finished the first, and longest, of the five "major prophets."

# DAY 37

## DIRTY JOBS

*[Scheduled Reading: Jeremiah 1-17]*

There was a TV show called, *Dirty Jobs* where host Mike Rowe took on the most difficult, strange, disgusting, or messy occupational duties.

**When I think of the biblical prophets, I think of the ultimate "dirty jobs." Prophet work was downright dangerous...even deadly.**

Confession: I went to Wikipedia for these facts, but check out the fate of some of the prophets:

> ➤ Isaiah suffered martyrdom by being sawn in two by King Manasseh (and Manasseh is in the line of Christ!)

> ➤ Jeremiah suffered martyrdom by stoning at Tahpanhes in Ancient Egypt

> ➤ Ezekiel suffered martyrdom in the land of the Chaldeans

> ➤ Some of the minor prophets were martyred as well (i.e. Micah, Amos)

**Prophets were special men and a special resurrection awaits them one day. (The heroes in Hebrews 11 understood the special prize that awaits those who suffer for God in this way).**

Jeremiah's calling speaks to the amazing sovereignty of God.

The Lord tells Jeremiah, "Before I formed you in the womb I knew you, and before you were born I consecrated you; I appointed you a prophet to the nations." (1:5)

**This gives me a special appreciation for the prophets. We owe it to their lives to read their accounts.**

What a special privilege this 60-day Bible read gives us, the opportunity to honor these fallen prophets for their "dirty work" by reading the very words that they themselves received from the mouth of God.

# DAY 38

## CONTEXT

*[Scheduled Reading: Jeremiah 18-34]*

**One of the cool experiences about power-reading through the Bible is the opportunity to gain "context."**

While cruising through Jeremiah you'll encounter a familiar passage:

*For I know the plans I have for you, declares the Lord, plans for welfare and not for evil, to give you a future and a hope* (v29:11).

It's one of the most famous and frequently quoted verses in the Bible. But it has deeper meaning for those who have been reading through the Old Testament.

For nearly 38 days we've been reading about the journey of The Seed: starting with Adam... and eventually Noah... then Abraham.... then King David...

And now even after the kingdom has been divided (the southern and northern split), and both kingdoms have been captured, **God wants His children to know that He has their future in his control.**

God wants the Israelites to know that after 70 years of exile are complete, they will be restored to their place. (Sure enough, that happens - remember Ezra and Nehemiah?)

It's all part of keeping his promises to his chosen nation. And keeping The Seed alive.

# Day 39

## OBEDIENCE...AND MORE DIRTY WORK

*[Scheduled Reading: Jeremiah 35-50]*

I love the story of the Rechabites (Jeremiah 35).

God picks out this family and has them tested to see if they would drink wine. But the sons uphold the traditions and teachings of the family forefathers and refuse the wine.

**God uses the Rechabites to make a point to the Israelites - The Rechabites have obeyed their father about drinking wine, *but you (Israelites) don't obey me (God)!*** [v14]

Meanwhile, throughout the rest of today's read we see more "dirty work" for prophet Jeremiah. As a writer myself, having to rewrite the entire scrolls doesn't sound fun.

(Yeah - the king burned the first set of scrolls).

Next Jeremiah is imprisoned, and cast into a cistern where he sank into the mud (Jer 38:6).

More dirty work for the prophet.

**Seeing Jeremiah's life in this context helps me to better appreciate his obedient legacy.**

# DAY 40

## GROUNDHOG DAY

*[Scheduled Reading: Jeremiah 51-52, Lamentations, Ezekiel 1-13]*

**Jeremiah ends with a brief account of the fall of Jerusalem and exile to Babylon. Yes, we've read this account several times now.**

(Sort of feels like the movie Groundhog Day, doesn't it?)

Lamentations includes a set of poetic laments concerning the fall of Jerusalem. The author is not confirmed, but many suggest it was Jeremiah.

**Ezekiel seems to be next man in the prophet relay handoff, from Jeremiah, and his account begins just five years into the exile period.**

The prophet commissioning experience in Chapter 2 and 3 reminds me of the prophet Jeremiah. It's a dangerous job.

Ezekiel is God's "watchman." If he is not careful in serving his watchman duties, God would hold him responsible for the wickedness of others.

What a heavy calling.

**Strangely, there was a problem in those days with false prophets (Chapter 13), as there are today.** I'm not sure why anyone in those days would want to pose as a false prophet given it's dirty and deadly nature.

And guess what? You're at Day 40! For 40 days you've been reading the Bible in huge quantities.

Keep it up!

# DAY 41

## REAL PEOPLE

*[Scheduled Reading: Ezekiel 14-28]*

**Who would you say are among the most righteous men to have lived during the biblical era?**

Today's assigned read gives us a clue into God's mind on this.

In Ezekiel 14, God is making a point that judgment is coming for Jerusalem and no one can stop it. Even if three particular righteous men were found in Jerusalem, not even they would be enough to spare the city from God's wrath.

So who are these three special men whose names are mentioned by God?

**Noah... Daniel... and Job (v14).**

Pretty cool. The trio are referenced three more times in Chapter 14 (vv 16, 18, 20).

**For the astute Bible reader, the passage offers another random clue... Job is a real person.**

Remember on Day 25 I mentioned there's some chatter among skeptics and "theologians" about whether Job was real or a fictional person? **But this name drop in Ezekiel is strong proof that Job really existed in Biblical times.**

Okay, Bible-readers. Carry on.

And as we strive to walk with God, think of these great men - Noah, Daniel, and Job.

# Day 42

## I AM A WATCHMAN

*[Scheduled Reading: Ezekiel 29-45]*

**Ever since God routed The Seed through Abraham, God has appointed an overseer to lead the people spiritually.**

After the Israelites were led by Moses and Joshua, God assigned judges to lead. When the people rejected that system, God appointed kings to lead, with prophets serving in the background. **As the kings failed to follow God, he turned more and more to these prophets.**

Being a prophet was an intense calling. **When you read Ezekiel 33, notice the accountability God placed on Ezekiel - he called him a "Watchman." Ezekiel was tasked with telling the people everything God told him to say.**

If the people do not repent as a result of Ezekiel's warnings, the guilt was on them. If the people do not repent because Ezekiel has not warned them, God would hold Ezekiel responsible.

**As a father, I am a "watchman" to my family.** God may not hold me spiritually accountable in the same way He held the Old Testament prophets, but it helps me to think of my role as that of the family prophet.

**If you are a parent, you are a family prophet as well - a Watchman.**

Reading through the Bible and seeing the role of prophets is inspiring me to "up my game" as Watchman for the Anderson Family.

How about you?

# DAY 43

## DANIEL...A SPECIAL MAN

*[Scheduled Reading: Ezekiel 46-48, Daniel 1-12]*

**Remember Ezekiel 14:14, the mention of the righteous men, Noah, Job and Daniel?**

What's interesting about this trio is their respective time periods. Noah's flood was around 2349 BC. Job is believed to have lived 2150 BC. But Daniel was among the captives of the Babylon captivity in 607 BC.

**Daniel was a contemporary to Ezekiel, who began his prophet ministry in 595 BC.**

While Noah and Job's stories were ancient to Ezekiel - over 1500 years old, Daniel was a current day faith giant in Ezekiel's time.

The life and character of Daniel is enormously special. The legacy of he and his three friends is an awesome story of obedience and faithfulness, even to the point of death.

**This small book (Daniel) contains many of the famous Bible stories that are taught to children today... the fiery furnace, the handwriting on the wall, Daniel in the lion's den, Nebuchadnezzar's famous dreams.**

Then there's Daniel's own vision from God that fits in the eschatological studies alongside the book of Revelation.

The book of Daniel is a loaded book.

**After today's read, take a deep breath. Because you're now finally through the Major Prophets!**

# DAY 44

## DIRTY WORK – DIRTY MARRIAGE

*[Scheduled Reading: Hosea, Joel, Amos]*

**I like the minor prophets. They're short books. :-)**

The prophet "dirty work" continues. Hosea was ordered to take a whore as a wife, and have children with her. God directs him to name their kids with names like, "No Mercy" and "You are not my People." (Stories like these hardly seem real, but I believe them).

I am sure Hosea loved his precious babies named No Mercy and You are not My People. And perhaps that was the point. God loves His children, too. But He wanted Hosea to understand how much God detested their unfaithfulness.

And if that wasn't enough, God had Hosea redeem a wife from adultery. (We don't know if this is the same wife or a different one.)

**Once again, God used the prophets to undertake seemingly bizarre measures to help them connect with His message.**

And as an interesting observation in Amos 1:1, there's mention of "the earthquake." A quick google search suggests a massive quake that affected many cities during this period. This was likely the type of event that today would warrant full media coverage for days, weeks, or even months. But it gets two words mention in scriptures.

**History is vast. And noteworthy events have occurred all throughout history. But the bulk of the words in the Bible are devoted not to news - but to the things on the mind and heart of God.**

# DAY 45

## THE SEED MAKES AN APPEARANCE

*[Scheduled Reading: Obadiah, Jonah, Micah, Nahum, Habakkuk]*

A fun thing happened at church one Sunday when I was at around Day 45 during one of my previous Bible reads.

**My pastor was preaching on Micah 5. He started the sermon with the Bible's "Big Picture," from Genesis 3:15 - God's promise of a Seed that will defeat the serpent one day.** (Remember my notes on Day 1?)

Next, my pastor walked The Seed through Abraham, the man with whom God made the famous covenant - that he (Abraham) would become father of many nations.

Next he highlighted God's covenant with David - the promise that David's throne would endure forever.

Finally, in the day of Micah (during rules of Jotham, Ahaz, and Hezekiah), we have this golden prophecy:

*"But you, O Bethlehem Ephrathah, who are too little to be among the clans of Judah, from you shall come forth for me one who is to be the ruler in Israel, whose coming forth is from of old, from ancient days." (Micah 5:2)*

It's a forecast of the coming Messiah. Christ the King. The baby from Bethlehem.

**The prophets are full of sneak-previews of the coming Messiah.**

Those who studied the prophet scrolls had this to look forward to. And those on the other side of history have had these prophecies to look backwards.

One of those backward-looking teachers was Matthew.

In his gospel account, Matthew referenced several prophets in his opening chapters: Isaiah, Jeremiah, Hosea....and Micah 5:2 (See Matthew 2:6).

**We're right in the middle of the big picture!**

# DAY 46

## YOU'VE DONE IT!

*[Scheduled Reading: Zephaniah, Haggai, Zechariah, Malachi]*

**Congratulations! After today you will have finished the Old Testament.**

When you hold your Bible in your hand, you should be able to see how much you've read - and what little remains. The New Testament covers 14 days of the 60-day reading schedule.

**Before we close out the Old Testament reading, I want to plant a flag. It has to do with a topic on the last few pages of Malachi, The Book of Remembrance (3:16-18).**

This "Book of Remembrance" is essentially *The Book of Life*, a record containing the names of those who have been set apart by God, just "as a man spares his son who serves him" (Malachi 3:17).

It's a deep, serious biblical theme. One that surfaces again in the final pages of the Bible. Check out Revelation 20:12-15 and you'll see.

The name of everyone who has ever lived (born or unborn) has an identify and will be recognized by God in either the Book of Life, or in another set of books. Those whose names are in these other books (not the Book of Life), will suffer eternal judgment.

**Notice how God closes out the Old Testament in the same way as how the New Testament will conclude: a reminder of the coming judgment that awaits all of mankind.**

Malachi's book is small. But it's final message is HUGE.

# DAY 47

## HEAVEN

*[Scheduled Reading: Matthew 1-17]*

The 60-day read creates an interesting flow.

**For 46 days we've been slogging through the Old Testament while The Seed works its way through human history. Then in one day's read (today), Jesus is born and He launches His ministry.**

Tomorrow (Day 48) His earthly ministry will be over. From a Bible-reading perspective, the life of Jesus appears and passes quickly.

**While reading Matthew, notice a particular mega-theme: The Kingdom of Heaven.**

Matthew quotes Jesus' reference to heaven repeatedly throughout this book. **From the 4 gospel books, heaven is mentioned roughly 150 times. And 85 of those mentions are in Matthew.**

It's stunning to me how little we talk about heaven today in our churches, given the weight of attention it receives in the gospels.

Enjoy watching for this recurring theme as you read through Matthew.

# Day 48

## A BIZARRE STORY...THAT MAKES SENSE

*[Scheduled Reading: Matthew 18-28, Mark 1-3]*

In the last chapter of yesterday's read, (Matthew 17), Jesus took three friends up the mountain to show them a glimpse of his heavenly appearance.

In the first chapter in today's read, (Matthew 18) the disciples were asking Jesus, "who will be the greatest in the kingdom of heaven?"

**It's no wonder the disciples were intrigued by heaven, right?**

The mega-theme of heaven continues. Over the next several chapters, more parables explain the kingdom of heaven.

Finally comes the arrest of Jesus. Then the crucifixion. Then the resurrection.

**Here it is in a nutshell:**

> ➤ After 4,000 years of biblical history, our God comes to earth as The Seed.
>
> ➤ He's born a baby.
>
> ➤ He grows up a man.
>
> ➤ He dies as a slaughtered lamb.
>
> ➤ He goes back to heaven.

At first glance, it's a bizarre story.

**I recently read this quote: "Christianity is the only major religion to have as its central event the humiliation of its God."** (*Church History* by Bruce Shelley).

But for those of us tracking the biblical narrative for 48 days, it makes perfect sense. This is just one huge benefit of our reading.

# Day 49

## INSPIRED ANCESTRY

*[Scheduled Reading: Mark 4-16, Luke 1-3]*

**Today's read ends with a powerful genealogy of The Seed.**

Luke Chapter 3 lists every generation from the 1st Adam (in the Garden of Eden), to the 2nd Adam (Jesus Christ).

77 generations in all.

While Luke details the Seed's path through Mary, Matthew Chapter 1 presents a partial Seed path from Joseph to King David.

(Both Mary and Joseph can trace their descendants to King David: Mary through David's son, Nathan; Joseph through David's son, Solomon).

**These two chapters (Matthew 1 and Luke 3) are treasures to historians in helping to verify the ancestry of Jesus.**

As a young child I accepted the story of Jesus Christ and have trusted it ever since. I didn't need much proof. (That's one of the blessings of being raised in a Christian home.)

But as an adult today, it's comforting to know that the ancestry of Christ can be traced all the way to the beginning.

The works of the gospel writers were brilliantly inspired by God!

# DAY 50

## EVERY STORY HAS AN ENEMY

*[Scheduled Reading: Luke 4-16]*

**Along with heaven, there's another recurring theme we see in the gospels.**

Demons.

As Jesus went about healing the sick, He cast out demons, too. Jesus had a particular affinity for helping the demon-possessed.

For much of my life, as I have read the Bible, my eyes pretty much leaped over any mention of demons - almost like they were metaphors for evil.

I don't fully understand these beings, how they operate, and how they exist around us. But I know they're real. (And there's some fear in that!)

In Luke 8 we have the famous story of when Jesus cast the demons into the pigs. **What's particularly fascinating about this encounter is how fearful the demons were at the sight of Jesus.**

After all, they recognized Jesus. They knew exactly who Jesus was. They know who their true enemy is - Jesus! And they know the fate they will meet at His hand.

(And there's comfort in that!)

In ten short days (Day 60) you'll be reading Revelation. Chapter 12 details the war in heaven in which Satan and his angels were once cast down to earth.

Demons are real. Dark spirits are real. Satan's force is real. He knows his time is short (Rev 12:12), and that's the reason he wages war against your soul, and souls of your family.

**Throughout the gospels and the rest of the New Testament, pay attention to references to this spiritual battle between good and evil.**

This battle lies at the very core of the Bible's narrative set out in **Genesis 3:15**.

**The Seed from the woman is going to be harassed by the serpent for a while longer. And then one day in the future (see Revelation).... POW!**

The story's getting close to the end, folks.

# Day 51

## WHY ARE YOU READING?

*[Scheduled Reading: Luke 17-24, John 1-5]*

It's tricky reading the four gospels in just seven days.

The stories, parables, and events start running together. You think you just read a certain story, then it shows up again. You wonder if you already read that particular day's reading, then realize you haven't.

**That's why I've marked Mark & Luke as Speed 2 reads.**

But I want to create a speed-bump (that's means a reflection moment) for us at John 1:1-2.

*"In the beginning was the Word, and the Word was with God, and the Word was God. He was in the beginning with God."*

The passage feels like a tongue twister - or maybe a riddle.

Verse 14 gives us the clue, telling us that *"the Word became flesh and dwelt among us."* **The Word is Jesus.**

John is telling the reader that this book is about the man who is God. He has existed since the beginning of time with God.

Therefore, whatever He said can be trusted.

I trust one of the reasons you're reading the Bible is because you value its inspired, authoritative source. **Reading the Bible is the most direct way to access the very heart and voice of God.** The Bible is the only tangible item we have to represent God Himself.

Somewhere on a mountain rests the remains of Noah's ark. And somewhere lies the ark of the covenant. And various museums have various artifacts that come from Biblical times.

**But the Bible is the most authentic representation of God's voice and very being that exists. And we have the honor of reading it.**

Think about that as you read through the gospel of John.

# DAY 52

## PRAY FOR THESE TWO THINGS

*[Scheduled Reading: John 6-17]*

**Today's read concludes with a powerful example for a praying parent.**

Jesus is hours away from heading to the cross. His betrayal and arrest is imminent. The 4,000 year Seed-journey is about to be completed.

Jesus offers a final prayer for his disciples. Think about what this prayer means: his last moments of quiet and solitude before chaos would erupt in Jesus' life.

You could say the future of his ministry rests heavily on these final prayers for his spiritual offspring. He does not pray for safety from physical harm. He does not pray for protection from persecution or even from death.

**What does Jesus pray for?**
**Two requests (see John 17:15, 17).**

Protection from the evil one (v15) - Just as the demons recognized Jesus, He was keenly aware of their existence. Jesus respected the threat the evil one posed to the disciples and He wanted "soul protection" for His followers.

That God would sanctify them in the truth (v17) - Next to protection from evil, Jesus knew that more than anything else, the disciples needed to remain rooted in truth. *Your word is truth*, Jesus acknowledges before God.

These two powerful things. Protection from evil. Sanctification in the truth. That's my prayer for my children.

# DAY 53

## PROPHECIES FULFILLED

*[Scheduled Reading: John 18-21, Acts 1-8]*

**In today's read alone, we encounter the fulfillment of four special prophecies.**

First, some context.

In the Old Testament, God installed three religious festivals for the Israelites, consisting of seven separate feasts. Because we're reading quickly and didn't have time to study these in-depth, here's a helpful list:

> ➤ Passover Feast
> ➤ Feast of Unleavened Bread
> ➤ Feast of Firstfruits
> ➤ Pentecost (Feast of Weeks)
> ➤ Feast of Trumpets
> ➤ Day of Atonement
> ➤ Feast of Tabernacles

Each of these feasts are loaded with symbolism. And each are prophetic. Between John 19 and Acts 2 (five chapters), these four feasts are fulfilled:

> ➤ Passover (Christ's death on the cross)
> ➤ Unleavened bread (Christ died without sin)
> ➤ Feast of Firstfruits (the resurrection)
> ➤ Pentecost (the coming of the Holy Spirit)

What about the remaining three feasts? Those are still yet to be fulfilled and are connected to end time events (rapture of the church, Israel's returns to Christ, the millennial kingdom on earth).

**Being on this side of history, we have the benefit of seeing that certain prophecies were fulfilled, and can be confident in the ones that remain ahead.**

# DAY 54

## READING BEFORE UNDERSTANDING

*[Scheduled Reading: Acts 9-28, Romans 1-3]*

I love the story of the Ethiopian Eunuch in Acts 8. (It's part of yesterday's read, so I'm double dipping.)

An angel sends Philip to a location where he finds the man reading from the prophet scrolls - the book of Isaiah.

Philip asks the man "Do you understand what you're reading?"

To which the Ethiopian replies,

"Of course not!" (Jeff's paraphrase).

**Here's what I love about the story. The man was reading the Bible even though he did not feel confident in his understanding.**

That's ME!! And you too, right?

I began my Bible reading many years ago when I did not have full confidence in my Bible knowledge. But God has taught me along the way.

I suspect you also began this 60-day journey with some insecurities of your own. But you kept reading anyway. And think of how much have you learned.

Understanding God's Word starts with reading... period.

I'm proud of all you 60-day Bible readers!

**A quick note about the book of Acts:**

Paul's journey sets the stage for the rest of the New

Testament writings. After Acts, just twenty-two New Testament books remain.

Eight of them are written by Paul - another five are believed to be ascribed to him in some way.

As you read Acts, and Paul's letters, notice all the "dirty work" endured by Paul - arrests, trials, beatings, and scorn.

Sound a lot like the lives of Old Testament prophets doesn't it?

# DAY 55

## STUNNING TRUTH

*[Scheduled Reading: Romans 4-16, 1 Corinthians 1-9]*

**Guess what? You're 90% through the Bible read. Just six days remain.**

For me, Romans is the most difficult New Testament book to power-read.

It seems I have to read each verse at least twice to really get it. Paul's philosophical approach to explaining the gospel is rich... meaty... but sometimes confusing.

I do believe he breaks a lot of grammar rules at times with his long sentences, extra commas and dashes to support his zig-zagging thought patterns.

Romans is a great book to circle back around to later for deeper reflection.

One particular passage that stands out to me is in Romans 9.

God's sovereignty is stunning. God *has mercy on whomever he wills, and he hardens whomever he wills* (v18). Paul reminds us that God is the one who chooses who will know Him... who will resist Him... who will pursue Him, etc.

For the age-old debate of God's sovereignty vs man's freewill - Paul seems to take a position. Sovereignty wins (9:16).

**Among the major themes that run throughout the Bible, one that has had my full attention is the one of God's sovereignty.**

When you get to Revelation (you're almost there), take particular note of Rev 13:8. You know the Lamb's book of life that has the names? It was written *before the foundation of the world.*

**Your name was inked in the Lamb's Book of Life before the foundation of the world.**

**God's sovereignty is stunning.**

# DAY 56

## FLYING HIGH...AND LOW

*[Scheduled Reading: 1 Corinthians 10-16; 2 Corinthians 1-13]*

For 56 days, we've been flying high - looking at the scriptures from skyscraper levels.

**But today's read reminds me of a season in my life where God had me reading the scriptures at ground zero, on my hands and knees, with my nose in the grass.**

The verse I read was 2 Corinthians 8:12. Paul is preaching on financial giving, specifically about what he called an acceptable gift.

I thought about that verse for a few years. Eventually I left my position with a global ministry and started my own ministry called *Acceptable Gift*.

From there God led me on a very deep-dive study on the theology of giving. Going all the way back to the gifts of Cain and Abel, I peeled the onion in answer to my questions: *what kind of gifts are acceptable to God? What kind of gifts are not acceptable? How does God see our gifts?*

The end result was a stack of notebooks in my office containing my research on the gifts of the Bible, including a thorough study of the Old Testament sacrifices.

Out of this effort came a book called *Plastic Donuts: Giving that delights the heart of the Father.*

Five years later, over 30,000 copies have been shared in churches across the continent and even beyond.

I've really enjoyed my power readings of the Bible over the past year. It's opened up a whole new way of experiencing God's Word.

But this reading experience should not replace the need for me to dig deeper and look closer at God's texts at the micro level. A simple verse (again, 2 Cor. 8:12) changed the trajectory of my life and ministry calling.

And you likely have a signature verse or two that has deep meaning for your life.

**God's Holy Word is vast. It's mind boggling to think of the global collection of Christian works and changed lives as a result of a single verse or passage of scripture.**

Okay, let's get back up into the air. We're about to land the Bible-read soon but still have a few more days to go!

# DAY 57

## PATIENT FAITHFULNESS

*[Scheduled Reading: Galatians, Ephesians, Philippians, Colossians]*

There's a tendency to think that Paul (formerly Saul) had his conversion experience, then hit the road as traveling missionary and whipped out a bunch of letters.

But that's not the case.

While Paul did begin some preaching right away, he kept a low profile, too.

Some of his letters came 10-20 years or more after his conversion experience. A few verses in Galatians give us a hint. Let's take a look:

After his role persecuting Christians, and then his Damascus road experience - Paul *"went away into Arabia, and returned again to Damascus."* (Gal 1:17)

*Then after three years....* (Gal 1:18)

*Then after fourteen years...* (Gal 2:1)

So here we have at least 17 years on record before his letter to the Galatians.

This tells us Paul's letters are the result of many years of careful study, observation, teaching, learning, and revelations (yes, visions from God).

All the more reason we can trust them.

If Moses was the author of the foundational books of the old covenant laws, Paul is the one who reconciles them to the new covenant.

What better candidate would God choose to reconcile the old to the new, than one who was a fanatic of the law...one who knew it frontwards and backwards?

As you read Galatians, Ephesians, Philippians, Colossians - you're reading from one who understood the law... and spent decades learning to unravel and communicate the mysteries of the gospel.

Paul understood he had been set apart before birth (Gal 1:15) for this very purpose. And he stewarded his calling well, wouldn't you say?

# DAY 58

## THE END IS NEAR

*[Scheduled Reading: 1 & 2 Thessalonians; 1 & 2 Timothy; Titus; Philemon]*

It's official - we're near the end. Just three more days.

I'll begin my wrap-up now. Because when "Day 60" hits, it's Revelation... and then it's over.

**While Revelation signals the end of the Bible story, we get plenty of hints of this ending in Paul's letters.**

Like the Revelation of Jesus Christ to John, Paul must have also had some spectacular visions from God. (He hints at these visions in subtle ways throughout his books. See 2 Corinthians 12:2 for an example.)

In 1 Thessalonians 4 & 5, Paul speaks of the rapture... and the Day of the Lord. And read closely 2 Thessalonians Chapter 1. Notice the theme of angels, flaming fire, judgment, punishment, destruction.

**Paul was motivated by the end times events, and wants us to be also.**

**End times are a reason to persevere, to hold to godly living, to live out God's calling on our lives, to guard our doctrine, to beware of false teachers, to run for the prize (all Paul's words, not mine).**

As you finish reading Paul's letters, take note of his sense of urgency. Paul speaks as if the end times are near... just as Jesus did.

# DAY 59

## MORE... OF THE END

*[Scheduled Reading: Hebrews, James, 1 & 2 Peter]*

Hebrews Chapter 11 - it's one of my favorite chapters in the Bible.

**It's known as the "Faith Hall of Fame" chapter - a roll call of faith heroes who lived life looking ahead to a reward. A reward yet to be received when they died.**

(That means they were looking forward to their reward in heaven.)

Some of the unknown faith heroes referenced endured extreme persecution and fatal outcomes in exchange for these rewards.

They were stoned, they were sawn in two, they were killed with the sword (Hebrews 11:37).

Remember, the prophet Isaiah was one of those who was reportedly sawn in two. (See Day 37 blog, *Dirty Jobs*)

Like Romans, Hebrews is another great book to circle back around to later for deeper reflection.

2 Peter is another "end time" themed book. Guard your salvation, make your calling and election sure, watch out for false prophets, be ready for the day of the Lord.

Sound familiar?

These are Paul's themes also.

**Peter, like Paul, was one of the central figures in the book of Acts and both suffered much for their witness. It reasons that they would share the same vision, hope, and urgency for the end times.**

Ok friends, we're really at the end. After today, just one day remains. And what an exhilarating read it is!

# DAY 60

## COMING SOON

*[Scheduled Reading: 1, 2 & 3 John; Jude; Revelation]*

**The first time I read the full Bible in this power-reading fashion, Revelation hit me like a freight train - jolting my spiritual senses and reminding me how serious God's plan really is.**

Revelation is really a short book. But something about reading it in one sitting makes it come alive. I don't have to understand all the symbolism and eschatological events to benefit from the read.

There's plenty to understand that's in plain English.

Yes, it's dark... and dreary... frightening... and sad... It's all those things.

But in God's view, his wrath and judgment is just... and it's coming! (Soon, by the way.)

After 20 chapters of dreadful judgment, death, blood, battles, plagues, etc. - we finally come to the end (which is really the beginning).

After death and hades (that's hell) are swallowed up in the lake of fire, the new heaven and new earth appear (chapter 21).

We get the dimensions of the New Jerusalem (that's going to be like heaven's capital city). We get a blueprint of the city and it's precious materials - streets of gold, gates made of giant pearls. And there's the tree of life, again (remember, from the Garden of Eden?).

Kings from the earth will bring their splendor into the gates. Pretty cool.

Be sure to note the final Chapter 22.

**Three times, Jesus says *His* return will be soon (verses 7, 12, 20).** Jesus is coming to reward those whose names are in the book of life (v12).

And there's a special blessing in store for those who read and keep the words of the prophecy of this book (verse 7). All the more reason to make sure we read this book on a regular basis.

**As Bible readers, we have now read the entire Bible. We have seen all the prophecies that have been fulfilled. And we can know that the ones that remain (in Revelation) will come to pass as well.**

Friends, it's been an awesome privilege to walk these sixty days with you. There's much to process from it all.

I have a few more thoughts to share on these next few pages to help us soak in this great journey. For now, take a deep breath. And do something to celebrate what you've just accomplished.

**You just read the entire Bible... in 60 Days. Wow!**

## CONGRATULATIONS! YOU'VE DONE IT.

But what's next for your journey? First, I'd be honored to receive your feedback about the experience.

Second, I've put together what I call, *The Five Pillars of Biblical Literacy*, in the appendices that follow. I believe they will also help to develop a framework to know God better through His Word.

And just as important, these pillars will help you lead your family and articulate your faith to others.

Jeff
www.JeffAndersonAuthor.com

# YOUR TURN

Tell me about your experience with this book and the 60-Day Power Read, I'd love to hear from you.

Subscribe to my newsletter and receive updates and resources for your walk with God.

www.JeffAndersonAuthor.com

If you're interested in having me speak at your event, or want to host this 60-Day Power Read experience at your church, please contact us. Bulk pricing is available.

*The results of the 60-Day Bible Read Experience in the lives of our people was life-changing. The living and active Word of God, coupled with Jeff's guidance through its pages, is a powerful force!* —Pastor Eric Bryan, Fellowship Bible Church

# ABOUT JEFF ANDERSON

Jeff Anderson speaks and writes about walking with God with an approach that combines scripture and story. He's the author of two books, *Plastic Donuts* and *Divine Applause* (Multnomah/Random House). Jeff and his wife, Stephanie, have four children.

WWW.JEFFANDERSONAUTHOR.COM

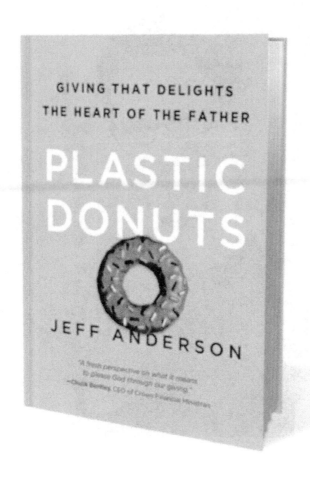

GIVING THAT DELIGHTS
THE HEART OF THE FATHER

PLASTIC
DONUTS

JEFF ANDERSON

"A fresh perspective on what it means
to please God through our giving."
—Chuck Bentley, CEO of Crown Financial Ministries

PLASTIC DONUTS IS THE STORY OF A SPECIAL
GIFT THAT HELPED ME TO SEE GIVING FROM
GOD'S PERSPECTIVE.

Instead of bringing us closer to God, and each other, the topic of financial giving is murky for most believers.

This is why I wrote *Plastic Donuts*.

The message is the result of my deep-dive study of roughly 2,000 gift mentions in the Bible. *Plastic Donuts* takes away the awkwardness that so often accompanies the subject of giving, and replaces it with biblical clarity.

Contact us about free group-study resources, sermon notes, and campaign materials.


*Jeff Anderson is a longtime friend. He is highly qualified to share the principles and practices of generosity with others because he personally lives them. Want to become more generous? Learn how from Acceptable Gift.*

—Chuck Bentley, CEO, Crown Financial Ministries

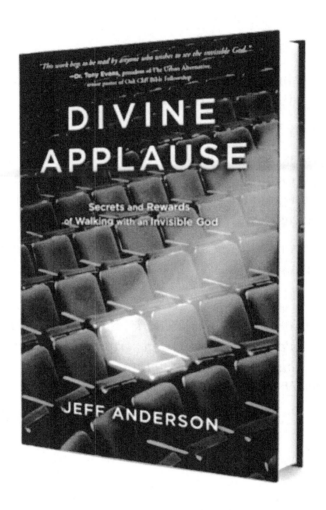

"This work begs to be read by anyone who wishes to see the invisible God."
—Dr. Tony Evans, president of The Urban Alternative,
senior pastor of Oak Cliff Bible Fellowship

# DIVINE
# APPLAUSE

Secrets and Rewards
of Walking with an Invisible God

## JEFF ANDERSON

HOW DO WE HAVE A RELATIONSHIP WITH A
GOD WE CAN'T SEE?

It's tough being separate from God, and even tougher because we don't know what we're missing.We can't hear His voice or see the Fatherly love in His eyes.

Or can we?

- Experience God's attention in unmistakable ways

- Cultivate an awareness of God's presence

- Enjoy the reward of secrets between you and God

- Take risks to break out of a status-quo life and connect more personally with God

- Discover how God is intensely interested in *you*

You don't have to settle for a silent or distant relationship with God.

*God is invisible. At last we have a book that addresses this reality in a creative, refreshing, and encouraging manner.*

—Dr. Richard Blackaby, author of *Unlimiting God,* co-author, *Experiencing God*

*This work begs to be read by anyone who wishes to see the invisible God.*

—Dr. Tony Evans, President, The Urban Alternative. Senior Pastor, Oak Cliff Bible Fellowship

JOURNEY OF THE SEED

CATCH THE BIBLE'S BIG PICTURE IN 60 DAYS

This reading challenge takes you from Genesis to Revelation with four important features:

- A focus on The Seed - the ancestry from Adam to Jesus

- A daily Bible reading plan yielding about one-third of the Bible

- Daily guidance and insights along the way

- Discussion points for you and your family

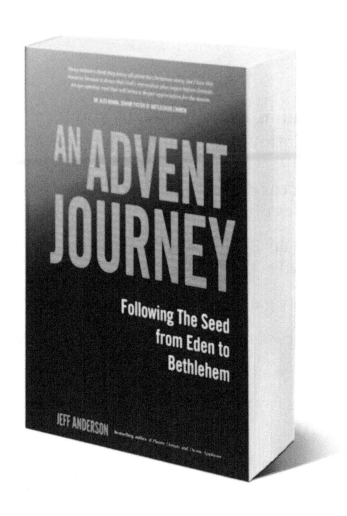

AN ADVENT JOURNEY

FOLLOWING THE SEED FROM EDEN TO BETHLEHEM

You and your family can discover the big picture of the Bible through this eye-opening, daily reading.

In just five minutes per day, discover the real story behind the Christmas story.

# My Notes

Made in the USA
Coppell, TX
05 April 2020

18540879R00108